l masterfully navigates the sacred ter-
rain where words falter but the spirit speaks volumes. This
book is a compelling exploration into the depths of spiritual
communication, where silence and the soul's yearnings co-
alesce to form a powerful conduit for divine intervention and
transformation."

Alan DiDio, founder, Encounter Ministries

"*Wordless Prayer* is an invitation to every believer and intercessor whose heart cry is to abide in Him in the secret, intimate
place. You will be awakened into a journey of a surrendered
and intercessory prayer life. One deeply in tune with His presence from dedicated times of entering into His throne room
and encountering Him in His glory. Discover how He hears
and be empowered into victorious breakthrough."

Rebecca Greenwood, cofounder, Christian Harvest
International and Strategic Prayer Apostolic Network

"Tammie Southerland is a woman of great passion and great
prayer who knows the depths of pain and heights of hunger
that compel a heart into intercession. She offers an anointed
call to a generation to go deeper into intimacy and intercession.
Highly recommended!"

Billy Humphrey, director, GateCity Church

"I have known Tammie Southerland for more than a decade,
and her passion for Jesus and desire to see the bride equipped
in prayer and intimacy with Him are contagious. It is my joy
and honor not only to recommend this read, but also to en-
dorse Tammie's life and ministry."

Jeremiah Johnson, founder, The Altar Global and Five Fold
Family Church Leadership Network

"I believe there is a prayer on the other side of words that God is awakening in this generation. He is delivering us from plastic, superficial prayers and is ushering us into something born of God that brings forth the purposes of God. God is awakening mothers and fathers in the Church who have had to walk this out in very personal ways, and Tammie Southerland is one of these mothers. *Wordless Prayer* is a prophetic call to come into those groanings of the Spirit Paul talked about in Romans 8. It's here where the will of God is made manifest in a generation. I've known Tammie for more than ten years and can attest to the purity and desperation that bleeds through every one of these pages."

Corey Russell, author, *Teach Us to Pray* and *The Gift of Tears*

"Tammie's heart groans for the Lord, and it is reflected in her desire to seek Him and teach others how to access those depths of intimacy to carry the kingdom in the earth. *Wordless Prayer* holds the keys to help you access those depths in God!"

Dr. Candice Smithyman, host, *Glory Road* TV show and *Your Path to Destiny* on It's Supernatural! Network, CandiceSmithyman.com

WORDLESS
PRAYER

WORDLESS
PRAYER

HOW GOD HEARS AND ANSWERS
YOUR GROANS AND TEARS

TAMMIE SOUTHERLAND

Chosen

a division of Baker Publishing Group
Minneapolis, Minnesota

Published by Chosen Books
Minneapolis, Minnesota
ChosenBooks.com

Chosen Books is a division of
Baker Publishing Group, Grand Rapids, Michigan

Printed in the United States of America

Library of Congress Cataloging-in-Publication Data
Names: Southerland, Tammie.
Title: Wordless prayer : how god hears and answers your groans and tears / Tammie
    Southerland.
Description: Minneapolis, Minnesota : Chosen Books, a division of Baker Publishing
    Group, [2024] | Includes bibliographical references
Identifiers: LCCN 2023048347 | ISBN 9780800772567 (paper) | ISBN 9780800772574
    (casebound) | ISBN 9781493445691 (ebook)
Subjects: LCSH: Prayer.
Classification: LCC BV245 .S628 2024 | DDC 248.3/2—dc23/eng/20231213
LC record available at https://lccn.loc.gov/2023048347

Cover design by Rob Williams

Baker Publishing Group publications use paper produced from sustainable forestry practices and postconsumer waste whenever possible.

24 25 26 27 28 29 30   7 6 5 4 3 2 1

This book is a blazing tribute to the unsung intercessors and fiery messengers—those who have been overtaken by God's very heartbeat in unceasing yearning for His fullness. You've carried a burden beyond words, an ache beyond human description. You've felt exposed and misunderstood in prayer meetings, church services, and the tapestry of society, much like Hannah, firmly rejecting the enticement of worldly pleasures. This dedication is a rallying cry for those who lack the human vocabulary to convey the burning grip of the Holy Spirit's voice within—an unspoken anthem that roars and longs that others would share in the splendor of His incomprehensible beauty.

and

To my mother and father, who—when they didn't know what to pray when their daughter was deeply lost—travailed in tears, groaned, and cried out for God to "rip her out of the clutches of Satan." The tears you cried and prayers you prayed had a ripple effect that snatched not only me but future generations from the enemy's grasp.

May the Lamb receive the reward of His suffering.

Contents

FOREWORD

LANA VAWSER

God invites us as His people into a sacred place to carry His heart and His groans. To carry the burden of the Lord is so intimate and holy. What a deep privilege it is to partner with Him. In this hour the Lord is not only awakening His people to their authority in Him, but also stirring us to carry His heart in intercession with purity, integrity, humility, and sensitivity.

There is a fresh wind of the Holy Spirit beginning to increase in intensity, convincing His people that we are *all* called to pray. We are *all* called to be houses of prayer that house His heart, His groans, and His burdens with a fiery, ferocious focus that is violent in the spirit because we are living before His face. Daily, as we behold His beauty and His majesty, we are being overcome repeatedly by the magnitude of His power, moving His Church from living on the defense to living on the offense.

Wordless Prayer, scribed by my beautiful friend Tammie Southerland, is a gift and a weapon for the Church in this new era. The Lord has given Tammie such wisdom to help the body of Christ move deeper into the governing place of intercession through her personal experiences, encounters, revelation from the Lord, and divine insight.

As I read these pages, I felt the invitation of the Lord to come up higher and the commissioning of the Lord upon His Church to extend His kingdom through intercession.

It is an absolute privilege and honor to carry Jesus's heart and be invited into the divine birthing room of His plans and purposes for His Church and the earth. We also have the responsibility as God's people to steward His heart with reverence and awe of who He is.

As you journey through these pages, Tammie will equip, teach, impart, and release to you heavenly insights and tools for this new era in partnering with Him in intercession and wordless prayer.

I see fresh hunger for Jesus coming for you as you are awakened in greater ways to your authority in Christ. He wants you to see His kingdom come—and His divine order, justice, glory, and majesty revealed in the earth for such a time as this.

It's time to ascend in intercession, to see as He sees, and to govern in unprecedented ways from your heavenly seat in Christ. Be prepared to be marked by fire and gripped with His groans in a greater way as you read. I was.

Lana Vawser, Lana Vawser Ministries; author, *The Prophetic Voice of God, A Time to Selah,* and *I Hear the Lord Say "New Era"*

Acknowledgments

Daymon Southerland: My love, my husband, who has loved me like Elkanah loved Hannah through the years of deep groaning and yearning for more than any human could offer me. You wanted to give me ten times the earthly blessing, but I refused to be satisfied with the pleasures of this world. Though you didn't fully understand the burden, you loved me deeply and moved where the Lord charged us to go. Words will never express how thankful I am for you. You are the love of my life.

My Inspirers—This Book Is about You

I saw your faces while writing this book. You have been struck with the unspoken groan yet longed to know how to express the deep cry within. You wanted to know if this weight is "unto something." This book was written as an intercession and guide for you to know you aren't crazy. You are radically in love and one with the heart of heaven. You are changing history with your prayers.

To my daughters, Eden, Jayden, and Aldey Southerland, and to Jessica Southerland and all the Southerland sisters marked with a groan, and to Paul and Emily McRae, Crystal Hornbeck, Sandi (Mom) Southerland, Rhema Trayner, Theresa Pridgen, Amy Lyle, Jeff Lyle, IHOP–Atlanta/GateCity intercessors, and many others who I've encountered who long to understand the wordless: Burdened ones, you inspire and drive me. This book is about you and for you.

Imparters and Intensifiers of the Groan

To Corey Russell, Jeremiah Johnson, Sarah Coker, Billy Humphrey, Wayland Henderson, Tom Ledbetter, Demetria Stallings, Lana Vawser, and my Pink Incense Ladies: Thanks a lot for messing me up and increasing this burden every time we get together.

Acknowledgments to Special Editors

Virginia Bhashkar and Valerie Smith, I could not have done this without you. Thank you for your work under pressure.

1

UNSPOKEN INTERCESSION

As the deer pants for the water brooks, so my soul pants for You, God.

—Psalm 42:1

Lightning-like jolts pulsed through my body, my heart racing as I was shaken from a deep sleep. I sat up in bed, and the tangible glory of the Lord penetrated the darkness. I couldn't see Him, but Jesus was in the room. His voice seemed to resonate from within and outside me as He spoke a single word: "Unspoken." Suddenly, I recalled a name: John Allen Chau. I pondered with Him the word *unspoken* and this recently martyred twenty-six-year-old missionary. *How do the two connect?*

As the voice of the Lord reverberated through my spirit, soul, and body, He was unveiling a mystery and a message that He wanted me to embody. In the early morning darkness, I was frantic to understand the full meaning of God's message. As a minister, an intercessor, and even a mother ever seeking new depths of connection with Jesus, I'd learned He never

15

spoke mysteries only so I could share them with someone else or preach a great sermon. His messages are intentional. He invites His friends into unspoken mysteries, things unseen and veiled to the world, so that we may know Him intimately and be transformed by these holy grippings.

This encounter on November 18, 2018, left me temporarily speechless, and the truth that God had connected His word to a martyr quickly filled me with a sober-minded fear of the Lord. I knew very little of John Allen Chau before three o'clock that morning; he had been killed on North Sentinel Island only about twenty hours before this encounter. I'd seen responses to the tragedy on social media, ranging from condemning Chau for illegally going to the island to praising him for laying down his life. Chau was gripped with compassion for an unreached tribal people on a remote island in the Bay of Bengal between Southeast Asia and India. In his journal, he expressed this simply to his family: "You guys might think I'm crazy in all this but I think it's worth it to declare Jesus to these people."[1]

While commentators argued in the news and on social media about Chau's actions, I tried to piece together what the Lord was unveiling. I was baffled by the single-word clue, and I struggled to understand the Chau piece until I began to connect this experience to a life-altering duo of encounters I'd had with Jesus in Israel earlier that year.

My visit to Israel had been my first official ministry trip outside the US. It was Pentecost and the seventieth anniversary of Israel becoming a state. The nation excitedly welcomed Americans as the US embassy had officially been moved to Jerusalem. Previously, I'd received countless invitations to minister in other nations, but the Lord had always told me to refuse the offers and to wait on Him.

The alignment of this trip was a setup for me to be Holy Ghost–bombed by the Lord. The moment I arrived, my innermost being was burning as if Jesus were welcoming me to His homeland. I knew I would return to the States a different person.

It all began in the Garden of Gethsemane, which was reserved for our team's private use for one hour to pray alone. The aim was to tarry with Jesus in prayer as the disciples did, and although they had failed, we were excitedly determined to succeed. While there, we often wondered how they fell asleep as the Messiah wept and groaned in prayer the night He was arrested. The atmosphere was oddly tranquil, but the scene, beautiful. The fragrance of rosemary filled the air, and beautiful purple flowers were scattered about, but the most shocking sight was the ancient olive trees in full bloom, bearing beautiful olive fruit on that day in May 2018.

I scanned the garden, looking for a place to sit with Him, full of expectancy and waiting for Him to lay me on my face. I spotted a bench, nestled away from the walking path, where I sat with Bible in hand. I breathed out and said, "Here I am, Lord. Let the encounters begin." Then, I felt absolutely nothing. Yes, that's right—nothing at all for a full forty-five minutes. I flipped through the Bible and tried to pray, but my mind wandered, and I could not land on a passage. In frustration, I exhaled a raw prayer, "Jesus, what is going on? This is the garden of all gardens! I hear people all over, sniffling and weeping in their encounters with you! Speak, Lord! We only have fifteen minutes left here."

Then, Jesus broke the silence and asked me one direct question: "Tammie, do you want more?" No tongues, glory, or fireworks, just a sudden, weighty, breathtaking question. He had invited me into a spiritual wilderness of agreement with Him, challenging me to count the cost before giving my answer. Would I tarry with Him in this hour through end times, even if it cost me my reputation, ministry, and life? My response manifested as tears, transcending all words, though I felt a holy understanding that He perceived my heart's reply.

Not wanting to leave the garden, I reluctantly moved toward our next location and the second Jerusalem encounter that would forever change me. My steps were unsteady, and His presence continued to envelop me Spirit to spirit. Eventually, we reached the entrance of Caiaphas' pit, where Jesus had been held captive after His arrest after enduring flogging and brutality in the Roman courtyard just hours before. Descending the dim concrete stairway, I attempted to regain my composure as faint rays of light filtered through what seemed to be a small window.

Suddenly, my friend tapped me on the shoulder and pointed at a circular aperture above our heads, barely wider than the circumference of my body. He whispered, "That's where they lowered Him down."

At that moment, a gut-wrenching travail erupted from within me as I saw Him. His face, battered and nearly unrecognizable, was adorned with a crown of thorns. His lips moved, but no human language emerged. Nevertheless, His voice permeated every dimension of my being, and I once again sensed His cry. "Tammie! Do you desire more?"

My only response was travail, tongues, and tears. I found myself speaking in Hebrew while a friend began to sing, leading to an outpouring of worship and the declaration of Scripture within the pit. I remained undone, prostrated on the cement floor, listening intently for His voice. Then He revealed, "I could have left this pit at any moment, but I surrendered my life in the garden of travail hours before they confined me here." He gave His life through intercession, uttering to the Father the words "Nevertheless, not my will but yours be done."

Those heated summer experiences in Israel intensified my craving for heaven to meet earth. I knew by "more," He was talking not about more fame or a larger ministry platform but about brokenness, tears, groans, and being misunderstood and mistreated yet increasing in the knowledge of His mysteries, beauty, and deepest desires.

As the days turned to weeks, I realized that in the twilight hours of that cool November 18 morning, God had catalyzed the unveiling of the mystery of the "wordless groaning" of Romans 8:26, which says, "In the same way, the Spirit helps us in our weakness. We do not know what we ought to pray for, but the Spirit himself intercedes for us through wordless groans" (NIV). God was helping me see Chau's struggle to verbalize the supernatural force within him that compelled him to become a faithful witness to the Sentinelese people. His family, friends, and professors could not understand. He was driven. Words were inadequate; he just had to go. Just as Jesus was obedient to His Father, even to the point of death on the cross, our suffering with Him involves aligning ourselves with His desires and promises and being willing to tarry with Him during times of profound darkness.

As my own journey into the unspoken continued, I became more radically obedient to the Lord and, like Chau, more misunderstood. The whirlwind of challenges included the closing of my ministry base; confusion among friends and family; acquiring, struggling, and rising in a new ministry position; the near death of my daughter; and experiencing immense loneliness and heartbreak. But over the next four years, I came to understand and embody what it means to abide in the throne room while lacking language to express the inner transformation and new conception in my soul. I learned that God marked me with something wordless long ago, gripping me with every facet of what is inexpressible.

I've discovered that amid the groans and tears—the wordless holy frustration between *what is* and what *should be*—God meets and beckons us more deeply into Himself. Remembering how the disciples failed to recognize the hour and fell asleep, we must contemplate our response when He offers us more in this present hour. This "more" that He invites us into is a commission to live the lifestyle of a fiery messenger, burning with His presence and purpose.

In the depths of our souls, where the Spirit of God intertwines with our being, exists a profound and mysterious language of groaning. This language surpasses the limitations of human words and transcends the boundaries of our understanding. It is a divine melody woven into the fabric of our existence, connecting us intimately with the heart of God.

In this groaning, you may encounter moments of deep longing, unutterable yearning, and aching for the fullness of God's kingdom to be realized on earth. It is a sign of your spirit aligning with the heartbeat of Jesus, resonating with His eternal desires. You may find yourself groaning for justice, mercy, and the restoration of all things, echoing the cries of creation itself. In these groans, the seeds of transformation are sown, birthing within you a faithful witness and intercessor of the power and glory of Christ. That power of wordless groaning, mentioned in Romans 8:26, could explain why followers of Christ willingly risk everything for God. Through the travail of groaning, you are being transformed into a faithful witness to shine the light of Christ in a world longing for redemption.

Let's explore the identity formation of the prophetic child of God through intercession. In Christianity, we identify as God's children by our sonship (Romans 8:12–17), in our everlasting union or friendship with Jesus as a bride (Ephesians 5:32; Revelation 22:17; Isaiah 62), and in answer to the Great Commission as messengers (Matthew 28:16–20). Further, Spirit-to-spirit intercession also empowers as it exposes the reasoning mind to the immortal, eternal identity.

For this perishable must put on the imperishable, and this mortal must put on immortality. But when this perishable puts on the imperishable, and this mortal puts on immortality, then will come about the saying that is written, "DEATH HAS BEEN SWALLOWED UP in victory. WHERE, O DEATH, IS YOUR VICTORY? WHERE, O DEATH, IS YOUR STING?"

—1 Corinthians 15:53–55

As we abide in prayer, we become people who are not of this world but living testimonies of Jesus. Yielding to the silent wails of the Spirit leads us to encounter the desires of Jesus and aligns us with the prayers of heaven: "The Spirit and the bride say come" (Revelation 22:17). Once formed as true witnesses by our proximity to Christ, we are obliged to preach with audacity what we have seen and heard. We no longer share the story of Christ historically but as those who experienced Him personally.

Lovesick Surrender and Friends of the Bridegroom

The Lord uses our groans and prayer to draw us into a lovesick hunger from the inside out. This deepens our friendship with Christ as it develops our willingness to surrender everything for the cause of love. But first, we must be willing to be uncomfortable and nurture a longing for God such that it makes Him our one unquenchable desire. We must answer the groan of all creation (Romans 8:22), trusting the Spirit to help us when we're struggling. The Lord's glory will surely cover the earth at the end of the age, as even in their wordlessness, His children respond to the cry of His heart to step up and take their rightful place.

We know that the whole creation has been groaning as in the pains of childbirth right up to the present time. Not only so, but we ourselves, who have the firstfruits of the Spirit, groan inwardly as we wait eagerly for our adoption to sonship, the redemption of our bodies. For in this hope we were saved. But hope that is seen is no hope at all. Who hopes for what they already have? But if we hope for what we do not yet have, we wait for it patiently.

In the same way, the Spirit helps us in our weakness. We do not know what we ought to pray for, but the Spirit himself intercedes for us through wordless groans. And he who searches our hearts knows the mind of the Spirit, because the Spirit intercedes for God's people in accordance with the will of God.

—Romans 8:22–27 NIV

Consider John the Baptist, who was gripped by God from the womb. As we'll explore later in detail, John faithfully yielded to the all-encompassing forerunner call. Understanding the burden of the Lord was more than preaching a message of repentance. He called himself a friend of the Bridegroom: "The bride belongs to the bridegroom. The friend of the bridegroom stands and listens for him, and is overjoyed to hear the bridegroom's voice. That joy is mine, and it is now complete" (John 3:29, BSB). John understood friendship with Jesus included listening for His voice, obeying even unto death—yet walking in holy joy and being captivated by the mysteries of heaven.

Could yielding to His sovereign intercession awaken and unveil His imminent return and unblock the understanding of the secrets of Scripture?

Perhaps wordless prayer is similar for you and me. Could yielding to His sovereign intercession awaken and unveil His imminent return and unblock the understanding of the secrets of Scripture? Could wordless prayer bring new levels of spiritual formation that transition servants of God into lovesick friends of God?

Mysteries Manifested

Paul said in Colossians 1:26 that "the mystery which was hidden [from angels and mankind] for ages and generations, but has now been revealed to His saints (God's people)" (AMP). Human words cannot adequately express how Jesus loves His friends and longs to reveal mysteries to them and do eternal works in and with them.

Everyday people—like Abraham, Elijah, the prophets, Hannah (the mother of Samuel), Moses, Mary (the mother of Jesus), Elizabeth (the mother of John), John the Baptist, John the Beloved, Mary of Bethany, Joan of Arc, John Wesley, John Allen Chau, Tammie Southerland, the teary-eyed intercessor at your church, the roaring preacher on your social media feed, and you—have been branded with an unearthly seal of eternal longing for more than what can be seen or heard with our carnal senses.

So often, those who enter the depths of wonder and get glimpses of the heart of God seem wild, untamed, and risky—in a holy way. These recklessly abandoned lovers of God are willing to become undignified, say the unthinkable, and even die so that Jesus's glory and story will be made known in the land of the living. Jesus is not some mute idol; He is our God and friend: "The secret [of the wise counsel] of the LORD is for those who fear Him, and He will let them know His covenant and reveal to them [through His word] its [deep, inner] meaning" (Psalm 25:14 AMP).

Jesus reveals mysteries to His friends in ways that go deeper than words in a similar fashion to covenantal marriage or time-tested friendship: "I have called you friends, because

Jesus reveals mysteries to His friends in ways that go deeper than words. all things that I have heard from My Father I have made known to you" (John 15:15). The closer a couple becomes, the fewer words are needed. They share an unspoken *knowing* between them. They have a history with one another. Mysteries are not so mysterious between lifelong lovers. When something is not spoken, it is thought, felt, expressed, or understood without being directly stated.

Likewise, as our relationship with the Lord deepens, history is built with Him. He can speak yet use no words, or He comes close like He came to Moses, breath-to-breath and face-to-face, "just as a man speaks to his friend" (Exodus 33:11). This knowledge should at least provoke us to hunger. Unspoken, wordless groans are more than prayers in tongues or unspoken secret prayer requests. They are mysteries unveiled in layers between lovers. One unearthly Lover draws the earthly into a pursuit while taking up the longing for which there are no words in perfect intercession on her behalf.

Unveiling the Father's mysteries is one of the Holy Spirit's favorite adventures. He loves to make communication seven-dimensional. On this side of eternity, we define complete understanding as seeing in 3D, but in Scripture, the number seven—seen fifty-four times in the book of Revelation alone— defines physical and spiritual perfection.[2] The book of Revelation *is* the unveiling of Jesus. Simply put, there is so much more to be revealed when we seek to know Jesus through prayer in His Spirit.

As we grow in hunger and intercession, we will know Jesus as "the express image of [God]" (Hebrews 1:3 NKJV). We will gain an inner understanding of He who is "the Word who existed in the beginning, [and] became flesh and dwelt among us" (see John 1:3, 14). Beloved, Jesus is the Father expressed to us by demonstration (John 14:9). Jesus is Creator (John 1:2). He is the Gospel message and messenger (John 11:25). He is the Spirit of prophecy (Revelation 19:10). Jesus laughs, cries, weeps, groans, and lives the story He wrote before the world began. He is "the author and the finisher of our faith" (Hebrews 12:2 NKJV) and "the Lamb slain before the foundation of the world" (see Revelation 13:8).

Our Father hasn't changed the way He expresses Himself. His words are more than language or pages in our Bible; they are alive and create life. He forms His message in living vessels. When you groan with Him in intercession, He is making you His witness. Any true mouthpiece of God endures a lengthy period of spiritual formation before they can preach the Word of God as an actual eyewitness. Spiritual foundation that does not engage the unspoken realm of God is built on sinking sand. Suppose we do not embrace a lifestyle of prayer or chase after all of God. In that case, we become powerless blind guides (2 Timothy 3:5; Matthew 15:14). The pursuit of God becomes ever deeper through the adventure of holiness contained in the weight of intercession. Deepening our knowledge and becoming a witness requires intimate, proven, personal history with God.

As you press into Him in times of fervent prayer with holy gripping filling your heart, you are encountering One who is love. He is giving you His desires, His love, and His commission.

Crazy prayers are sometimes internally known, but externally, you can hear only groans. From somewhere deep within, you expel out of your belly: "I want to see like you see and feel what you feel. I want to be your hands

Wordless groans are more than prayers in tongues or unspoken secret prayer requests. They are mysteries unveiled in layers between lovers.

25

and feet. I want to know you as you know me. I must get closer to you." When this begins, your spiritual eyes are opened. You will soon see what He sees, feel what He feels, and long for His mercy, justice, and redemption.

You are becoming aware of the power of the unspoken intercession. He has secrets to disclose and understanding to share with you. There is great purpose in being apprehended by Him. Those like John Allen Chau were gripped and sent out when the Spirit's groan captivated their souls. You are about to find yourself in an abandoned pursuit of Him. You will feel lovesickness, frustration, holy hunger, dissatisfaction, and zeal for His house, but you will simultaneously be absolutely enthralled. God wants to equip you. He sees you, and He has branded you for this generation. Bearing the burden of the Lord is not exhausting but glorious as you learn how to stay yoked to Him.

LET'S ENCOUNTER

In the depths of your groaning, remember that you are not left to navigate this mysterious journey alone. The Spirit of God intercedes on your behalf, translating your groans into prayers that intertwine with the heart of the Father. Your groaning becomes a sacred symphony, harmonizing with the rhythm of heaven and aligning you with the purposes of the kingdom of God.

Sit still with the Lord. Silence the noise and turn your attention to the Spirit of God within you. Luke 17:21 says the kingdom of heaven is within you. You do not have to strive to enter His presence. Romans 8:26 takes the pressure off you to pray for you know not what to pray. Simply ask Him to awaken the groan of His Spirit. Ask Him to pray. Pay attention to the thoughts in your head, the feeling in the pit of your stomach, and the lump in your throat. Holy tears are trying to break through. He is stirring up the groan of the Spirit—deep, intense, out-of-this-world love that summons heaven's will to manifest in the earth. Are you aware of His inner gripping now?

PRAY WITH ME

Jesus, I want to be saturated in the holy mysteries of you. Help me to patiently abide, never rushing to find the right words for others but provoking the true embodiment of your message through these wordless moments. Jesus, walk into this room. Awaken the unspoken within me. I want to talk intimately to you, like lovers do. I want to know your heart, your mysteries, and your longing. Baptize me in your Holy Spirit and fire and stir up your groans within me. Amen.

2

GRIPPED BY THE GROAN

Hannah was praying in her heart, and her lips were moving but her voice was not heard. Eli thought she was drunk.

—1 Samuel 1:13 NIV

Hannah, the mother of Samuel, endured years of barrenness. Her weakness made her a lightning rod for heaven. Unable to conceive naturally, Hannah's need catalyzed heaven's dream to manifest. Hannah was gripped by the groan. She embraced the burden of the Lord, yielded to wordless prayer, and unveiled a heavenly mystery. Her prayers were not pretty or peaceful. They were not religious or impure. She was not drunk with wine—as the priest thought—but intoxicated with longing (1 Samuel 1:13).

Hannah's cries were for the gaze of the eyes of the Lord—not her husband, not the priest, and not her rival. Her cries were for His leadership, His defense, His justice, and a gift

Hannah was gripped by the groan. She embraced the burden of the Lord, yielded to wordless prayer, and unveiled a heavenly mystery.

that she could consecrate and dedicate to Him and Him alone. (See 1 Samuel 1:12–16.)

Have you ever groaned or cried out in intercession and felt misunderstood? It's a glorious experience to be misunderstood or frustrated, as it magnifies your longing for heaven's vision to be fulfilled on earth. Yes, this unspeakable life of prayer can sometimes feel like a thorn in the flesh when you don't realize it is unto something greater. Paul the apostle spoke of the thorn in his flesh to the Lord in prayer, and what was the answer? "And He has said to me, 'My grace is sufficient for you, for power is perfected in weakness.' Most gladly, therefore, I will rather boast about my weaknesses, so that the power of Christ may dwell in me" (2 Corinthians 12:9).

These groans through the burden of God impregnate us with His will. Isaiah 66:9 declares He always finishes what He starts: "'Shall I bring to the point of birth but not give delivery?' says the LORD. 'Or shall I who gives delivery shut the womb?' says your God.'" Stand firm in the hope that the mystery of glory will come as the groan grips you; surrender in weakness to His prayers through you.

> But if we hope for what we do not yet see, we wait for it patiently. In the same way, the Spirit helps us in our weakness. For we do not know how we ought to pray, but the Spirit Himself intercedes for us with groans too deep for words. And He who searches our hearts knows the mind of the Spirit, because the Spirit intercedes for the saints according to the will of God.
>
> —Romans 8:25–27 BSB

Hannah's barrenness produced a groan that caused heaven to stop and respond. God's wonders were first revealed in her and then through her. She gave birth to the pure priest and prophet Samuel. What she birthed in weak prayer was planned by God and transformational for the nation of Israel. In Hannah's weakness, the Spirit was made strong. The Spirit of the Lord knew her heart and mind, and He moved within her. Eli the priest rebuked her. But he took notice and eventually came into agreement with her prayers.

> Then Eli answered, "Go in peace, and the God of Israel grant your petition that you have made to him." And she said, "Let your servant find favor in your eyes." Then the woman went her way and ate, and her face was no longer sad.
>
> They rose early in the morning and worshiped before the LORD; then they went back to their house at Ramah. And Elkanah knew Hannah his wife, and the LORD remembered her. And in due time Hannah conceived and bore a son, and she called his name Samuel, for she said, "I have asked for him from the LORD."
>
> —1 Samuel 1:17–20 ESV

The Lord struck Hannah with His dream, and it came to pass, but not without the stretching, groaning, and purification process of prayer and fasting. He was forming within her more than she could ever ask, think, or imagine. Soon her mourning would be turned to joy, and she would realize God used her to manifest the mystery of life from a barren womb.

The Inner Witness

As with Hannah, the inner witness of the Spirit imparts to you the strength to press through accusation, trial, and affliction. In the words of Paul, there is an unearthly drive to "press on toward the goal for the prize of the upward call of God in Christ Jesus" (Philippians 3:14). Why? Because quickened within each born-again believer, by the Holy Spirit, is the inner witness of adoption into the family of God.

> You have not received a spirit of slavery leading to fear again, but you have received a spirit of adoption as sons and daughters by which we cry out, 'Abba! Father!' The Spirit Himself testifies with our spirit that we are children of God.
>
> —Romans 8:15–16

Knowing your sonship evicts orphanhood and allows the Spirit of God to flow freely. A son or daughter of God joyfully burns the filthy rags of the former life and puts on clean clothing to live the life of destiny prewritten in heaven's books, now and forever. Beloved, this earth becomes your mission field because you are seized by the Spirit of revelation and understanding that you, whether male or female, are a son of the living God. The perspective of suffering becomes momentary and light affliction as your mind, will, and emotions submit to your spiritual access as a son or daughter of God.

> But when the time had fully come, God sent His Son, born of a woman, born under the law, to redeem those under the law, that we might receive our adoption as sons. And because you are sons, God sent the Spirit of His Son into our hearts, crying out, "Abba, Father!" So you are no longer a slave, but a son; and since you are a son, you are also an heir through God.
>
> —Galatians 4:4–7 BSB

The unspoken language of prayer connects you to your sonship in a deeper way, because no words can describe life as a citizen of heaven or the glory of engaging in conversation with God. Jesus expresses to Nicodemus in John 3:1–21 that he must be born again to enter the kingdom of heaven. Like for a baby newly dispelled from the womb's darkness, the Holy Spirit opens the spiritual eyes of each person born of the Spirit.

Becoming a Witness and the Power of the Blood

As you groan in the spirit, you are being transformed into a faithful witness. Becoming a witness involves a three-stage process that transforms your perspective concerning your testimony and suffering in this life. As you grow, the inner agreement with the Holy Spirit plays an active role in intercession, increasing your knowledge of God and understanding of redemption. This often leads you into wordless groans and witnessing great wonders. As the author of Romans explains in 12:1, we voluntarily become martyrs in both life and death by consecrating our lives and putting to death our appetites for the flesh to advance the cause of Christ.

In the second stage, you become an active eye-and-ear witness through your personal history with God, bringing the weighty truth to testify to your personal experiences. The Greek word for witness is *martureō*, similar to the English word for *martyr*, and when combined with the Greek pronoun *sym* to form *symmartyreo*, it conveys Romans 8:16, the inner witness given by God to the believer.[1] This agreement is linked to the quickening of spiritual knowledge and the realization that you have been born again and are a child of God.

In the third stage, our maturity as a witness embodies the faithfulness of Christ—steadfast even unto death. We too aim to be "faithful unto death" that we receive the crown of life as described in Revelation 2:10. This stage unwaveringly demands living our testimony, both in life and in the face of death, mirroring His resolute commitment, exemplified in Hebrews 12:2, where we're urged to fix our eyes on Jesus, the pioneer and "perfecter of the faith, who for the joy set before Him endured the cross."

The noun *mártyras* emphasizes an eyewitness testimony that cannot be recanted.[2] A true believer, armed with first-hand testimony of God, remains steadfast, even facing persecution or death for their unwavering commitment. This deep commitment mirrors Jesus's testimony within them, connecting them to an eternal truth, embodying His love and eternal devotion. The blood of the martyred witnesses establishes authority in an affidavit that cannot be silenced, even by death.

Those who are killed for Christ, like John Allen Chau, realize their blood has a louder and longer testimony than their words. According to Genesis 4:10, innocent blood cries out from the ground in supplication, pleading for justice and redemption. Hebrews 12:24 states that Jesus's blood continues to plead louder than Abel's blood. Moreover, in Revelation 6:10, we see that the blood of the martyrs still cries out to Jesus for the fullness of time and His Second Coming. Could it be that these passages indicate there is more to being a witness and intercessor than we previously thought?

As Jesus promised, His disciples stood before kings and had the opportunity to testify to the truth. Ancient martyrs triumphed because they boldly and publicly proclaimed the truth before Rome, the world, and God, even if it meant their deaths. These faithful witnesses were fascinated by something beyond what is seen here in this realm; they joyfully bore testimony by word, intercession, and suffering, sharing in Christ's crucifixion in life and death. Friend, are you fascinated like these? If so, as you grow as His witness, you are embracing the power of His blood, your testimony, and His invitation to behold Him in the unspoken mysteries of prayer.

The Groan of Justice

As your inner witness grows stronger, you realize you are an eternal being, set free from the chains of sin and death. When the Holy Spirit inhabits a mortal body, death is no longer feared as the end or a punishment. Instead, the hope of immortality, glory, and bliss is born of faith. Heaven is your realistic homeland.

Dr. Martin Luther King Jr. said, "If a man has not discovered something that he will die for, in a sense, he is not fit to live."[3] Have you watched the news or scrolled through your social media feed and encountered a story of intense injustice? Suddenly, you are gripped. You feel deep unrest, a longing for justice; you try to pray, but the burden is too much. You are gripped from the inside out; you don't have adequate words.

In some moments, the longing for full redemption shakes us to the core. Without words, you say to the Lord, "End this evil. You must do something. No, I must do something." But human words are inadequate. Tears seem to well up from inside your soul. You know the weakness of your prayers as tears roll down your cheeks; your belly tightens, and the wordless prayer begins. You are speaking to God spirit to Spirit. Like the prophet Isaiah, your cry is "I am weak and broken but nevertheless. Here I am, send me!" (See Isaiah 6:8.) According to Romans 8:21, creation itself will be set free from its bondage to decay and brought into the freedom of the children of God as we groan.

In an encounter like this, you forget your flesh as the Spirit's groan strikes you to the core. You begin to feel a portion of what God feels for the weak and broken; your desires are becoming His. Hidden and seeded within your spiritual re-birthing is a groan for greater glory and for the curse of sin to be no more (see Romans 8:22–23).

But the love of God drives us, not to seek vengeance but salvation and redemption for the lost and depraved. "Though I bestow all my goods to feed the poor, and though I give my body to be burned, but have not love, it profits me nothing" (1 Corinthians 13:3 NKJV).

Like Hannah, we must become lowly and weak before the Lord in prayer. Unspoken, wordless prayer drives us to repentance and brokenness and leads us to ask Him to impart His desires and solutions. Paul emphasizes love repeatedly in 1 Corinthians 13. The apostle is helping these new sons and daughters through a paradigm shift. They were once fear-driven, pagan Gentiles; now, they would become love-driven sons of the living God. Christ has saved these Gentiles, filled them with the Holy Spirit, and they wildly gave their lives to prayer.

Beloved, powerful intercession stems from a heart yearning for closeness with God. We must embrace vulnerability before the Lord. Often, frustrations, spiritual attacks, abuses, and pain can breed bitterness, even within our prayers. Yet, tearful intercession has the power to shatter these assaults and heal wounds inflicted by others. In the words of Bob Jones, "Weeping gets the witchcraft out of your eyes."[4]

As we embrace the cry for justice, let us open our hearts to both cries for redemption and the light of divine exposure.

"Beloved, let us love one another, for love is from God, and whoever loves has been born of God and knows God. Anyone who does not love does not know God, because God is love" (1 John 4:7–8 ESV). These groans and tears are gifts that mold you into a friend of God, one who exudes love, instead of being blinded by trauma and seeking revenge for wrongs suffered.

The Unveiling

In the unveiling of your true purpose, a son or daughter of God emerges, intensifying the battle between light and darkness as ordained in Romans 8:18–19 and John 1:5. You step into your authority as a son or daughter of God, and all creation is celebrating, but the enemies of God are enraged. You become His powerful voice and a vessel of His glory in direct opposition to rampant evil.

You realize you are called out from worldly culture to be consecrated, set apart as holy unto the Lord. This is cause to celebrate. The formation of the witness has begun in you.

Remember, Jesus is the faithful witness. The spirit of prophecy is awakening your soul, calling you into partnership with heaven to hasten the Day of the Lord. He is inviting you to know the manifest presence and the supernatural demonstrations of the kingdom of heaven on earth. Though these encounters are rewarding, your purpose in Him is considerably more potent than experiencing or knowing supernatural mysteries. Your purpose is to be *revealed*.

This word *revealed* appears in numerous places, with Romans 8:18–19, 2 Thessalonians 2:3, and Revelation 1:1 offering a comprehensive view of eternal unveiling, revelation, manifestation, and

> The kingdom suffers violence; the violent take it by force.

exposure. In the Scriptures above, the Greek word is *apoca-lypto*, the same word we use for the apocalypse.[5]

Today, as we pray, you and I are becoming history's spiritual giants. Jesus involves us in the climax of a grand heavenly production. This invitation is personal and end-time prophetic. Your journey with God is peppered with incremental revealings. The most significant unveiling of history occurs in the last hour, according to 1 John 2:18. If John said it was the last hour two thousand years ago, then you play an integral role in these last seconds.

> Children, it is the last hour, and as you have heard that antichrist is coming, so now many antichrists have come. Therefore we know that it is the last hour.
>
> —1 John 2:18 ESV

The end of the script looks something like this: Creation gets the answer to her travail, the sons and daughters of God are unveiled, the Antichrist is exposed, and three and a half years later, the Lion of the tribe of Judah splits the skies. Every eye sees Him and bows to Him as He is slaying the evilest ruler of history with the breath of His mouth. Remember, Jesus wins when times feel difficult. You are here for a reason.

Understand, this groan within compelling you to play a significant role in the redemption of creation will cause you to become spiritually violent. You are not just interceding for the sake of interceding. You are being unveiled.

Burning Messengers

Burning Messenger: You're a flame of fire on this earth. Your frustration is real, but remember, you're supernatural. Use that frustration to draw closer to the Lord. Let Him probe your heart, reveal more about Himself, and elevate your prayers. Embrace the tension between Scripture's promise and the world's shortcomings. Journeying with Jesus sanctifies. Trials deepen our connection to His heart, fostering holy grit. Yield to the Holy Spirit; let love transform you.

Once, determined to tame my tongue and to purify my reactionary response to accusations, I went on a word fast, vowing silence. But I was a newlywed, and my sudden silence offended my husband. In my zeal, I thought this would make me become holy, and I thought he was pressing me to sin by asking me to break my silence.

He pleaded for me to talk; I resisted, thinking my silence was obedience to the Lord and for our deliverance from vain arguments, pride, and control. My husband grew angrier, demanding that I speak. Well, I spoke, all right. Accusations flew from both sides, turning into a strife-filled word battle. Immature and religious insults were exchanged, yet the Lord was purifying us deeply. Unknowingly, our souls warred against the Holy Spirit for control.

Some would call my reaction to my husband's pressure being spiritually violent, fighting for obedience to the Lord, but being spiritually violent doesn't justify reactionary criticism or spiritual pride. It's about birthing something, like Hannah, something world-changing through trials, developing inner peace amid the raging storms, responding with the word of the Lord, and standing firm as we long for heaven to conquer evil. When you are in the burning of frustration and longing to be set apart from the world, remember, you're not trapped. Pressures are used to press you into the cross; crucify the carnal nature by the blood of the Lamb and rise higher.

Our souls need sanctification and restoration to love post-rebirth. Yet, we possess a wholly radical Spirit who teaches perfect love, holy reformation, and heaven-rending prayer. As you groan with Him, you learn to yield to Him and become His messenger, aligning heaven and earth.

Gripped by the Groan

Being gripped by the groan of the Holy Spirit is more than an action; it is a personal and prophetic embodiment. You are inwardly branded by a love beyond this earth and often lose your ability to describe the longing inside. You pray, and only sighs, pants, and tears come. In my personal experience, the intensity is progressive. As your proximity to Him increases, so does your tolerance for more holy fire. His longing is for you to ask for more; He wants you to know Him and His ways. Weeping intercession is a natural response to coming into contact with the One who is always mediating for you. This remarkable journey will teach you how to carry His burden rightly.

Notice the emphasized words in the passage below.

> Now in the same way the Spirit also *helps us in our weakness*; for *we do not know what to pray* for as we should, but the Spirit Himself *intercedes for us* with *groanings* too deep for words; and He who searches the hearts knows what the mind of the Spirit is, because he *intercedes for* the saints according to the will of God.
>
> —Romans 8:26–27, emphasis added

We carry His burden. We feel His groans. We get to pray, cry, and see Him move with power. We have a job to do with Him. But notice who is interceding. He intercedes for us because we don't know what to pray. Friend, when you groan in the gap, you manifest the kingdom. As fiery zeal increases, the Spirit of God burns your inner idols, the baptism of fire catalyzes the process, and wisdom increases with spiritual age and emotional trials. However, as spiritual sight develops, you realize your brokenness, depravity, and impurity. As a result, you also gain eyes to see corruption in the world and His struggling church. These open eyes can set you up to be bold and beaten. Stay close to His heart.

You Are an Alarm, Not a Jingle Bell

You are an alarm, not a cute little jingle bell. As time grows nearer to His coming, holy fire leads to accelerated growth, maturity, and clarity of purpose. But never forget that this gift to groan is to identify with His heart and to move heaven and earth into alignment with His kingdom will. You have stepped into a gift of intimacy and intercession. Boldness and humility can reside together in a vessel of His glory. Humility and holy anointing form from the anguish and constant willingness to forgive those who want to silence the alarm. Holy boldness grows as you ask Him for help. You will be more aware of the sound of His alarms as the intensity of the earth's labor pains increase. Suffering and the response to draw nearer to Him amid it all reveal glory in us. Groaning is like an intense birthing symphony, reverberating within creation, induced by the Spirit. It's a lovesick spiritual agreement between the bride and her Bridegroom, proclaiming, "He's coming, and He reigns."

> I consider that our present sufferings are not comparable to the glory that will be revealed in us. The creation waits in eager expectation for the revelation of the sons of God.
> We know that the whole creation has been groaning together in the pains of childbirth until the present time. Not

41

only that, but we ourselves, who have the firstfruits of the Spirit, groan inwardly as we wait eagerly for our adoption as sons, the redemption of our bodies.

—Romans 8:18–19, 22–23 BSB

The *Spirit and the bride say, "Come!"* And let the one who hears say, "Come!"

—Revelation 22:17 NIV, emphasis added

In Matthew 3:11, John decreased in his public ministry when illuminating Jesus as holier, greater, and mightier than himself. John expressed that the Messiah's coming would be with an inward submersion of fire and the Holy Spirit. God's weighty presence requires fiery cleansing to allow you to co-labor with Him under His glory. Your wonder increases as you are made aware of His nearness, but so does your anguish. You must ask for discernment to know the time and seasons and declare the Bridegroom is coming; subsequently, your longing to be with Him face-to-face will intensify. You comprehend sonship identity, but are awaiting the adoption ceremony and complete inheritance. This travail is the gap between what you know by the Spirit, God's promises, and what is amiss in our world. Jeremiah, the prophet of old, was known as the weeping prophet. Notice his lamentation as he groaned in this gap: "My anguish, my anguish! I writhe in pain! Oh the walls of my heart! My heart is beating wildly; I cannot keep silent, for I hear the sound of the trumpet" (Jeremiah 4:19 ESV).

Like Jeremiah, when you hear the sound of the trumpet, your heart beats wildly, and you cannot keep silent, neither in the heavens nor in the earth. The pain Jeremiah feels could be from realizing the word of the Lord would be rejected. Oh, how I know this inward dirge. But we must remember His nearness and voice are the gifts, not the promise or prophetic word we deliver. The closer you come to God's heart, the more your eyes see. The burning heart of God within awakens 20/20 vision in a spiritually blind world. Wordless prayer is our place of solace, for we know the work done with our Father never returns void. No one wakes up one day and says, "I want to be alarming in a sleeping culture." Why? Because no one likes an alarm clock when it wakes them from a deep sleep, but the closer you come to the Lord, the more you become a sound of awakening. You are not a jingle bell, my friend. You are more than someone with an intense prayer list; you are an intercessor and His messenger.

Fix Your Eyes on Jesus

Come up higher, fix your gaze on Jesus, and discover His manifest presence. Messenger, His face is your reward, and eternity is your finish line. You are delivered in His presence from mind-binding religious mindsets and people-pleasing behaviors.

I am praying this over us right now: Lord, increase our sensitivity to being led by your Spirit and make us one in you. Increase our generation of yielded intercessors; make us ones who will trust you, ask for knowledge of your will, and minister to you before we minister to man. Give us a roar in the heavens and make us an alarm on the earth. Rip out double-mindedness that would hinder our prayers, yet make us meek, compassionate, and humble, yet bold and fearless. Make us deliverers in our families, churches, neighborhoods, workplaces, and nations.

Friend, like Hannah, you are being gripped by the groan, embrace the burden of the Lord, yield to wordless prayer, and unveil a heavenly mystery that transforms your life, family, and world.

LET'S ENCOUNTER

Holy messengers will blaze into heaven with earthly anguish behind them, full of excitement to behold His glory. Let your temporal pains be like dust in the wind. Come up higher, fix your gaze on Jesus, and discover Christ's manifest presence. Messenger, His face is your reward, and eternity is your finish line. In His presence, you are free, and the groans of your heart are satisfied.

Faithful messengers are led not by the criticism nor the acclaim of man but by the Spirit of God. In this encounter, ask the Lord to fix your eyes on one thing: to see His beautiful, fiery eyes. Beholding Him is how you will stay humble and aligned with His leadership. Ask Him to overwhelm your heart with the ability to love as He loves, and ask the Spirit of wisdom and understanding to remind you that He—not you—is the answer to everyone's problems. In this, your humble wordless prayers and spoken words of truth change the course of history.

Shouldering the burden of the Lord requires you to be unashamed of the message you carry, pray, speak, and proclaim in sync with His voice. When you receive your eternal crown and hear the Father say, "Well done, my good and faithful servant," you will understand your position with Him in this age.

May love and correction flow: When He says no or yes, so do we.

PRAY WITH ME

Lord, increase our sensitivity to being led by your Spirit and make us one in you! Increase our generation of yielded intercessors; make us ones who will trust you, ask for knowledge of your will, and minister to you before we minister to man. Give us a roar in the heavens and make us an alarm on the earth. Rip out double-mindedness that would hinder our prayers, yet make us meek, compassionate, and humble. Gripped by the groan for your goodness, we long to be deliverers in our families, churches, neighborhoods, workplaces, and nations. Amen.

3

HOLY BURDEN CARRIERS

Whoever dwells in the shelter of the Most High will rest in
the shadow of the Almighty. I will say of the LORD, "He is my
refuge and my fortress, my God, in whom I trust."

—Psalm 91:1–2 NIV

Jesus has a way of leading us to Himself in our desperation. You
may have come to Him with a burden for a loved one, a broken
marriage, frustration with your pastor or church, or heartache
over child sex trafficking, abortion, or the sin that abounds in
this generation. Then, when you had no words left to pray, you
gasped, and He overtook you. When you were at your weakest,
the groan of the Spirit pierced your soul; it broke something in
you that may never be the same again, which is a good thing. If
you trust God with your burden, your suffering will become a
great anointing. He never asked you to carry this alone.

Holy Burdened

To be much *for* God, we must be much *with* God. Jesus, that
lone figure fasting in the wilderness, knew strong crying, along

with tears. Can one be moved with compassion and not know tears? Jeremiah was a sobbing saint. Jesus wept! So did Paul. So did John. . . .

Though there are some tearful intercessors behind the scenes, I grant you that to our modern Christianity, praying is foreign.

—Unknown[1]

The tears mingled with the holy burden will keep you tender, humble, and forbearing. John the Baptist carried the burden of the Lord well. He prayed, trusted God, and never watered down the message, even when faced with death. As the son of Zechariah, a priest in the lineage of Aaron, John was in the bloodline of the priesthood, but his priesthood looked vastly different from his father's. In the Old Testament, a priest like Zechariah ministered to the Lord and prepared sacrifices for the holy visitation of Yahweh. But God had gripped John, filling him with the Holy Spirit from the womb (Luke 1:15), and He used him to prepare for the most significant visitation of the Lord that the world has ever seen. In John, the priesthood of the old covenant moves toward Jesus, a signpost illuminating the long-awaited Messiah and declaration of His great high priesthood and kingship and the arrival of the eternal kingdom.

John probably did not have the language to describe the prophetic burden he carried. I am sure his burden was accompanied by tears as with the prophets of old. When he spoke, he probably felt his words did not sufficiently express what his spirit knew. I am sure he experienced the pain of rejection, the cutting feeling of being misunderstood, and the frustration of knowing the religious system was blind and full of pride. He might have thought, *This is senseless. They will not repent, no matter what I say.* Nevertheless, he cried out. This groan within his innermost being was wordless and drove him to give up all the pleasures of this world. He probably didn't fully understand his prophetic destiny; he was simply gripped and aware of the gap between the promises in Scripture and what the religious system had to offer. Did he have the language to explain the inner compelling to his parents or the religious leaders? No, but he yielded fully to the call.

The Spirit drove John into the wilderness, and he fulfilled Isaiah 40:3, calling, "Clear the way of the LORD in the wilderness; make straight in the desert a highway for our God." Eventually, his brethren, the Pharisees, the Sadducees, and others would ridicule him and call him a madman. Still, Jesus would declare him "the greatest man born of woman" (see Matthew 11:11). Even as John gained a following and disciples of his own, he reduced himself to make way for Jesus to be glorified; he was imprisoned and beheaded. Instead of comfort, popularity, worldly prosperity, and fame, he chose eternal destiny, truth, and heavenly rewards. Every messenger, like John the Baptist, must decide whether to be a voice of truth or compromise.

Charles H. Spurgeon put it this way: "He that does not find his ministry a burden now will find it a burden hereafter, which will sink him lower than the lowest hell. A ministry that never burdens the heart and the conscience in this life, will be like a millstone around a man's neck in the world to come."[2] Those called by God have each been given different measures of grace to carry the burden of the Lord. The weight of the message may seem heavy in this life, but in the next, we will be judged in proportion to how purely we testified to the truth. We must remain yoked with Him, or the weight of His glory will crush us.

Perfected by the Burden

Jesus said, "For My yoke is comfortable, and My burden is light" (Matthew 11:30). Maybe you are like me, but I look at this verse and say, "Really? Because I have certainly felt the weight of His burden." When I look at John, the early Church, and those living in persecution, I think, *That doesn't look easy.* Even our light Western affliction of staying true to the message can feel too hard to handle. When I feel the weight suffocating me, I ask myself, *Am I yoked to Him in the weight of His glory, or am I trying to carry a mission for Him on my own?*

When we lean into the burden of the Lord, we will probably be incredibly misunderstood and subjected to the not-so-holy fire. King David noted that as his zeal for the Lord consumed him, the insults of those who insult God fell upon him (Psalm 69:9). Remember, the Lord sanctions the times of mourning with Him. This lamentation and mourning allow us to experience a portion of His deep love, zeal for souls, and His longing for the purification of His bride.

God infuses us with Himself, banishing our weakness and beckoning His strength. As the quote often attributed to Lieutenant General "Chesty" Puller goes, "Pain is weakness leaving the body." Perhaps what we experience as burdened witnesses is our weak flesh burning under the fire of God. We feel His love removing our excuses and complaints, allowing us to roll up our spiritual sleeves and get the eternal job done. Taking on the burden of the Lord is not for the faint of heart. Take courage and trust Him with the burden because the God of perfect love can cast out all fear from your feeble body (1 John 4:18).

> **Perhaps what we experience as burdened witnesses is our weak flesh burning under the fire of God.**

Under His protection, you no longer need to be tormented by the fear of failure, slander, or even death.

> Who will separate us from the love of Christ? Will tribulation, or distress, or persecution, or famine, or nakedness, or peril, or sword? Just as it is written,
>
> "FOR YOUR SAKE WE ARE KILLED ALL DAY LONG; WE WERE REGARDED AS SHEEP TO BE SLAUGHTERED."
>
> But in all these things we overwhelmingly conquer through Him who loved us.
>
> —Romans 8:35–37

The burden of the Lord is your calling, but abiding in Him is your job description. It will increase as the day of His visitation draws near, but you are not alone. He desires for us to come to Him, to stay near Him. The weight of affliction is becoming the weight of His glory.

His Yoke Is Easy, Not Sleazy

Let me warn you; when we come under the burden of the Lord, we may sometimes fire off our new revelations like a loose cannon and be rejected by man or snatched up into ministry stardom. Friend, pray that the heaviness of the burden of the Lord increases and that you would have keen discernment and be firm in the fear of the Lord. Cry out that He would keep you humble and shut doors that would cause you to fall away from Him. The spotlight is not your calling; Jesus is who you are called to. The throne room is your greatest place of influence. Platform is not bad or good; it simply provides a different opportunity to lead more people to Him, but it can

His yoke is easy, and His burden is light. also be a pathway to spiritual arrogance, rejection, loneliness, and slander, and thereby, great testing.

I've experienced long seasons of hiddenness and great opportunities for public influence. In my pain, I decided I liked hiddenness much more than public influence. I would not douse the purity of the word of the Lord or hold back tears in worship or prayer. I was placed on platforms and then gossiped about and slandered behind closed doors.

The knowledge of this only increased the weight of my burden for God to bring forth a modern holy priesthood. I would not accept the sleazy burden of performing to gain favor and fame. Amid my journey, doubts and questions bombarded my mind. Through tears and prayers, I shed false expectations, learning to walk alongside the Lord. This realization made me more vigilant in shouldering the true burden.

Most have encountered the deceptive burden that arises from shouldering the weight of the world, the Church, or your relationships and the dance of trying to make others happy. But as we embrace the journey, pain molds and shapes the glory of Christ within us. Did you know that false burdens can cling to us because of some area of woundedness we have closed off to the Lord? When you experience ungodly pressures, it teaches you the importance of casting your cares on God, allowing Him to heal your past and walking in step with Him. You're able to rise above any need for accolades and renounce offense. As you draw near to Him in times of pain and confusion, you're learning to abide in your identity, walk in forgiveness, and carry His holy burden humbly, rightly, and yielded to Him. His yoke is easy, and His burden is light. His yoke is easy, not sleazy.

The holy burden of the Lord is not to be promoted for selfish gain nor is the voice of the Lord to oppress. Your ministry to others will flow from a lifestyle leaning fully on Jesus, knowing He is your calling and He cares for you. The longer you journey with the Lord, the more you will discern how to rightly carry the weight of truth. It can feel heavy when you are angry at the tendency of man to make a mess. Use this as fuel to stand in the gap for fallible people. Ask for His eyes, heart, and words as you pray. He is answering your groans and tears as you bring Him the wrong and the desire to make it right. Remember, Jesus is the greatest defender, and He is justice.

As you yoke yourself with Him in intercession, you cast on His shoulders the waywardness of this current culture. As He heals your heart and gives compassion, grace, and mercy, He lightens the load, fulfilling the promise that He will draw His children back to Himself.

He Will Shatter the Yoke

Isaiah 10:27 reveals a profound truth regarding how the anointing of the Lord possesses the power to shatter the yoke of bondage. The New American Standard Bible describes the breaking of this yoke as being due to "fatness." Remember, Jesus Himself declared that His yoke is easy and His burden light. This powerful imagery of a broken yoke signifies the growth of oxen, reaching such healthy maturity that their constraint can no longer contain them. Isaiah 10:27 represents the transformative effect of maturing in anointing, which advances us in the richness of the oil of spiritual provision, liberating us from the shackles of our carnal desires.

Through the endless oil of the Lord, we find liberation from the shackles of traumas, wounds, and fleshly cravings. The unhealed areas of our souls lead us to be misused or abused. In Him, we have access to everything necessary for a life of godliness and abundance. As we walk uprightly before Him, nothing is withheld from us, for He lavishly provides for us as declared in Psalm 84:11. Sadly, the harness that traps many keeps them from growing up in the Lord. Their feebleness is fortified by fears of failure, abandonment issues, pride, traumas, and places of lost hope. However, as we embrace the overflowing oil of the Holy Spirit and get honest with Him in prayer, the chains of bondage break, enabling us to plunge head over heels into our eternal destiny. As we break free and get fat on the truth of the Word of God, we grasp the goodness of the Lord. The enemy's bribes no longer sway us, for we know who we are. We won't settle for moldy bread that does not satisfy. We won't feel we have to fight for our rights, because no one can take anything from us; we have the fullness of the Lord. We will freely give, trusting the Lord that He is the eternal bread of life.

Trusting God on a Co-Mission

You and I are yoked with Him in this race. We get to hear His voice and be led and protected by Him as we trust His leadership. We speed up when He runs and slow down when He walks. As we abide in Him, He will show us where He is going and who He is ministering to. He delights in inviting us along and flowing through us, who are conduits for His love. We are collaborating with Christ in our burden bearing. As we learn to trust Him, prayer becomes joyful and exciting. We get to see Him move in the lives of those we otherwise would resent. This is the fun part. But when we run with the Lord, we must discern His pace.

Think of being yoked to Christ on His mission this way: You are connected to an ox to plow a field. The ox stands firm in his place, but you take off in a full sprint, so you break your neck. This is what it feels like running ahead of the Lord while yoked to Him. The opposite is true if He runs and you try to sit down. You are drug across the field, your body flapping in the wind, your face planted into the dirt. (I'm laughing at this image too.) It's a co-mission, beloved. The faithful witness who has revealed Himself is with you—in the joy and glory, and in the wailing, pain, persecution, and void. He is there when you look death in the face, but He is also in thrilling, laughter, and days of plenty. He's still alive to intercede and eager to show you His glory. (See Romans 8:34–39.)

Spiritual Endurance Rewarded

When the fire of God inwardly brands your soul, you step into something greater than you can imagine. You are sealed as His child, invited into wonder, mystery, and intimacy with Him. He is the reward. His voice, His presence, His secrets are your prize. Of course, you will slip and fall. You will be used and rejected, but there is so much grace for you. Over time, spiritual endurance, tenderness to His leading, and attention to His voice increase. Know this: Our spirits always agree with the Spirit of God, but our emotions, thoughts, and strong will are fine-tuned.

Friend, being with Him is not a place of striving but a place of wonder and humility. The labor is to enter into His rest by throwing off all ungodly self-talk, accusations, woundings, entitlements, and spiritual pride. We must learn to die so we can live fully in Him. Yes, it is difficult to master trust and being still when our flesh is still set on worry and

When the fire of God inwardly brands your soul, you step into something greater than you can imagine.

is screaming, "Feed me!" Remember, a dead man has need of nothing but eternal life. We cannot be where He is when we are fixated on the anxieties and worries of this world, for they cause us to lose sight of His Word (see Mark 4:16–17). Longsuffering with Him brings joy and peace because we're free from worry. He sees, cares, and has grand plans to involve us in and share with us. Remember, the nations are His inheritance. In this commission of intercession, He is fashioning our character and prayers in alignment with His. According to the Scriptures, we share in His authority as we are seated with Him, the authority that He gained through His suffering.

He's in the Silence

Have you ever been in a room where everything suddenly went silent and you knew that God was there? The most powerful moments of co-missioning, prayer, and worship are yielded to His sound. He's not always loud; sometimes, He's super quiet. Both modes are powerful; both are to be entered with complete trust. But these moments of stillness permeate your soul. He is not anxious for sound to fill the room, and you are frozen, too awestruck to move. You know He is the sound, and He is filling the space.

I sat in this place of deep inner stillness for several days when our daughter Jayden was in the pediatric intensive care unit (PICU) fighting for her life. Often in silence, Jesus has full reign over our emotions and can use us as a conduit for His healing power. In this place, we have to get out of the way. We are at our weakest physically.

I think of it like the other side of the Jordan River. In Joshua 5:1–12, the Israelites had finally crossed over the Jordan to take the promised land; they were met by Jesus and circumcised. They had just entered into enemy territory, and all the warriors were subjected to an embarrassing surgery; can anyone say *sitting ducks*? The only warrior who would win the battle was Jesus. That's what we cry out for, right? To be pure and holy and that He fights our battles. But we do not expect Him to expose our flesh, consecrate us, and use our weakness in the process. Most of us want Him to do the heavy lifting and make us look good.

When we learn to trust and remain seated with Him, we develop the ability to have one ear to heaven, hearing eternal conversations in the counsel of the Lord, and one ear attending to the moans for His justice on earth. We learn only to move when He commands us to do so and to trust Him in the holy hush, even when the situation appears hopeless. We recognize Him as the ultimate authority who shapes the course of history as well as the true prophet, priest, king, and miracle worker. Despite our limitations, we comprehend that we are merely instruments He chooses to work through. When we relax into our heavenly seat, allowing silence to envelop us, the sound of heaven rushes from within and around us. In this silence, we are astonished by the power that flows through us when we release worries and anxieties about fleeting circumstances.

The Unspoken Prophecy

Holy silence is loud and full of glory. Jesus will speak profoundly through a vessel who embodies intercession and abides in His stillness. He longs to reveal what is available to us when we learn to trust in the heavenly realm while exercising our ministry on earth. Once, I was baptizing believers after a powerful night of ministry. The power of God was supernaturally striking those who entered the water; they were being delivered and marked by God. There was a lot of noise around me. People were shouting, music was playing, and even the wind of the Spirit was blowing, but I was incredibly still, listening to what He was saying and trusting what He was doing.

Weeks later, I heard the testimony of a young lady after I gave her a prophetic word that struck her heart. She had viewed the baptism video and was stunned to see that my mouth was not moving. She contacted me to tell me that I prophesied over her in the baptismal, but no words were spoken. I was shocked. I knew I was standing in the throne room as I submerged each person, but this was a wonder. The voice of the Lord spoke through me in the unspoken realm, yet the woman heard each word perfectly even though I never spoke.

The Lord is inviting us to discover a higher level of prophetic existence by trusting and abiding in Him beyond the chaos of the flesh and the demonic battlefield. By learning to stay yoked to Him from the throne, we can unlock new realms of wonder. The power of prophecy is found in the stillness. Listening, watching, and embodying His message and His intercession.

Speed Bumps and Forked Tongues

"If you don't come, we die!" With tears running down my face, I cried out again and again from the ground, then from the microphone during the staff prayer. "Jesus, come! If you don't come, we *will* die." Prophetic intercession can seem a little insane. Hours before, I was in a quiet place. I heard Him and cried in silence. Sitting with Him and telling your mind and emotions to wait heightens discernment and revelation. I was praying with threefold meaning. It was a shout of maranatha, yes, but it was also a wake-up call, a cry, and a warning for *us*, the prayer movement. I wailed with the Spirit about our lukewarmness and our deep need for Him.

Boldness arose, and I took the mic to lead our prayer time. Without reasoning with my carnal mind, the Spirit opened my mouth to speak and pray through me in His interpretation in English. My wordless groans and silent positions from earlier were being translated as prophecy in the moment as I called the room to urgent repentance for our lukewarm living and into holy boldness and fearlessness.

The Spirit was declaring Revelation 3:16 in today's terms: "You can no longer remain as vessels swayed by the winds and waves of the political climate or new doctrines. You've stifled your prayer lives to align with the culture, and the spirit of the age is manifesting itself among you. You must get your eyes back on Jesus and long for His coming, or you will lose the fire of your faith as well as the next generation. I desire to restore you, but you must recognize your need for me, or you'll ministerially and spiritually perish." The Spirit cried out for a grand return, washing away sin and apathy within the prayer movement. Before granting words, He offered repentance, tears, and groans. The deep longing was for His gripping presence once more.

The groan of the Spirit is always multigenerational, as He always longs to unveil Himself in every era. If we will sit with Him in our heavenly seat, we will feel His pain, joy, and longing for our hearts to be fully engaged with His. Silent whispers of the Spirit of God will collide with subconscious human frustrations when we confess our helplessness without His intervention. We must allow our tears and tongues to flow freely, understanding that they are opening heavenly doors. In humility, we receive invitations into His heart and divine strategies in dire situations.

Through the burden of travail, we eventually arrive at the place of being fearless and so intensely intimate with God that all we care about is His face. This process begins with realizing we are on a journey, and the road has ditches, speed bumps, tragedies, attacks, twists, and turns. Second, on this road of experiencing His heart in intercession, we begin to understand lies we believed about who God is and that the attacks on our identity are accusations of the enemy, which are the most significant derailments we will face. Fortunately, he and his demons have no power unless it is given to them. In our spiritual formation, we learn that Jesus's intercessions through us are not only for others but for ourselves. As we yield to Him, we see how He took away Satan's authority and gave it to the sons and daughters of God through His crucifixion and resurrection.

When you learn to pace and discipline yourself, you can see beyond temporary afflictions and become like a child in your trust in the Lord. As the accuser's voice fades, you become aware that every attack is not directed against you personally but instead reveals the enemy's plans against the global bride. You acquire war room intelligence and precise prophetic intercession. The voice of your Father becomes crystal clear. You begin to take on His longing to evict the influence of evil from the earth. Injustice becomes less about you and more about taking hold of all Jesus gave His life to apprehend. When you begin to meditate on the Scriptures, pray them out, and dialogue with Him, revelation and glory will come, as well as holy frustration. You have started to grab hold of the groan of all creation. "We know that the whole creation has been groaning as in the pains of childbirth right up to the present time" (Romans 8:22 NIV).

LET'S ENCOUNTER

You are developing in prayer beyond using it to blow off steam or get your needs met. More than simply enjoying the presence of God on Sunday morning, you're becoming a vessel of His presence—one with authority on earth to manifest the will He has written in the scrolls of heaven. In these times of desperate prayer, a powerful spiritual formation is happening within you. You are becoming a true witness of Christ as you trust Him and yield to the groan of the Spirit.

Weep, friend, weep. Pray, purify your heart, and be a voice. No one said others would listen or that the burden of the Lord would be easy. But I assure you, your intercessions are striking directly at the kingdom of darkness.

PRAY WITH ME

Heavenly Father, grant me the courage to boldly stand in truth, knowing that I can break free from every yoke of bondage. I thank you for your anointing and commission to proclaim your word boldly, but I also realize your oil's purpose to spiritually mature me. I want to comprehend your spiritual richness and endless love. I declare that I will resist every tactic of the enemy that seeks to keep me bound by oppression, fear, and insecurity, and I will break the hold of any spirit or childhood wound that would cause me to seek fame or need to be applauded by men. I declare I am complete in you and protected by you. Take me into the realms of the spirit; cause me to know the beauty of being an intercessor who sees and hears but with the humility of one who recognizes the burden is yours. Keep me in lockstep with you. Flood me with joy and peace as you break every false burden. Set upon me the holy weight of glory as I learn to love humility. In the name of Jesus the Messiah, I proclaim freedom and holy confidence over my life. Amen.

4

YOU HAVE HISTORY
WITH GOD

To have found God and still to pursue Him is the soul's paradox of love.

—A.W. Tozer

In relentless pursuit of God, there is a fire in our souls that
refuses to be quenched. In the words of A.W. Tozer, "To have
found God and still to pursue Him is the soul's paradox of
love."[1] Is it possible to unravel the mystery of our deep longing
for God woven into the tapestry of a profound and intimate
history built with Him in years of fervent intercession? Could
years of answered prayer and promises yet to be fulfilled be
the currency needed in the most dire moments to bring about
the miraculous?

I call the space between what is and what should be the
gap from which we intercede. When you groan in the gap,
you manifest the kingdom. Likewise, your intercession in

the *chronos* manifests in *kairos*. Let me explain. The ancient Greeks had two different words for time: *chronos*, meaning "chronological," and *kairos*, meaning "deep time."[2] In the New Testament, *kairos* means "the appointed time in the purpose of God," or "the time when God acts." In Mark 1:15, the *kairos* unfolds, and the realm of God becomes imminent.

We live our daily lives in the ticking seconds of *chronos*, but when we pray, we step into a timeless encounter with the Almighty. God doesn't confine Himself to *chronos*; our daily intercessions, tears, and groans serve as continual offerings before His heavenly throne, bringing His kingdom and divine purpose into our very beings. He is holiness personified, distinctly beyond our earthly realm. In the intensity of my intercession, I've fervently prayed, "Lord, etch this prayer into eternity; even when I grow weary, remember it." I'm sure you've made similar impassioned promises to God, like, "I'll fast without ceasing if you'd just draw near," or "Oh God, I long to worship you day and night." But then, the prayer meeting ends, and you're hungry, sleepy, and looking for the nearest Waffle House. We absolutely need more grit. No need to worry. He has engraved those prayers in heaven, and when the time is right, they will yield a glorious harvest.

Altar Stones of History

In the PICU, everything felt unreal. The sterile, fluorescent-lit room was a world unto itself. Jayden, my daughter, lay there, battling septic shock and muti-organ-system failure. The Lord began His work months before that with intercession and a friend's dream, a dream that was so unsettling, it shook me to my core. This was a warning—a prophetic dream—of the enemy's plan to destroy her life.

In those endless hours, standing in that room, I prayed like her life depended on it. I fasted, refusing to leave until I knew that Jayden would have a life-altering encounter with Jesus. The dream felt like a relentless reality, and I was locked in a battle for her life and soul.

In the dimly lit International House of Prayer (IHOP)–Atlanta prayer room, I walked a trench around the room, travailing in unceasing supplication for hours. Then it hit me like a lightning bolt. The dream wasn't just about Jayden; it was about her entire generation. I was at war, not just for her but against a pervasive spirit that threatened countless young souls. I became an intercessor, a voice for mothers everywhere who cried out for their children.

Tears streamed down my face, and my heart burned with a profound conviction. "Lord," I cried, "don't let me forget what it's like to fight for another child's life as if it were my own daughter's." In that moment, zeal consumed me, and I laid hands on every mother in that room, acknowledging the war against the spirit of the age and the power of a mother weeping for her kids. "Lord," I shouted, "if you give me a billion souls, I'll give them all back to you. Hear the cries of the mothers!"

Little did I know the weight of those prayers. They weren't just words; they were etched in the heavens. Psalm 56:8 tells us, "Record my misery; list my tears on your scroll—are they not in your record?" (NIV). Those tears, those prayers, were part of a celestial record, held before the Almighty.

What's incredible about intercession is that it connects our earthly cries with the eternal. What we offer in the confines of time yields miraculous results in God's perfect timing. Looking back, I see my prayers went ahead of me and would manifest to heal my dying daughter. This would be a foretaste and confirmation that He would rescue an entire generation from this demonic battle for their lives and souls. In those moments of unrelenting intercession, we transcend the boundaries of time, bridging the gap between our world and God's eternal purpose. We are building altars unto the Lord, marking our history with Him.

Groaning for Glory and History with God

Upon arrival at the ER, the doctors told me, "She's dehydrated and in septic shock. Her organs and systems are failing." It was as if my physical mind could not receive panic, only peace. Fighting for her life during the pandemic had added confusion to the doctor's ability to make an accurate diagnosis.

But an unseen shield of glorious faith surrounded me. Words contrary to truth hurled toward me but simply would not penetrate my history with God. He had proven His promises concerning our daughter's destiny many times before. For many years, I have stood in intercession for my children. I have seen His healing power spare her life before, and I knew in the depths of my soul her life was not over. I knew her destiny and His faithfulness to finish the work He began. I stood in peace amid an array of words proclaiming death. These words bounced off the fiery shield around my mind. The prayers of saints all over the world were the weapons of war over her life. This battle would not be won by human might nor by power but by abiding, beholding, and trusting Him.

Kairos and a Mysterious Nurse Named Sydney

In our darkest hours, with my daughter's life on the line, the power of prayer, personal altar stones, and *kairos* timing

66

became our lifeline. Jayden's life teetered on the precipice as her organs shut down. It seemed as if Jesus Himself rode in on the sound of voiceless intercession. To be held in prayer in times of anguish is an astonishing experience. Demonstrations of His love and power transcend time and space through faithful warriors. These intercessions ravish the heart of God and compel Him to move. Unity in the spirit pierces the veil, as proclaimed in Psalm 133.

Let me lead you into the heart-wrenching days when an extraordinary nurse named Sydney entered our lives. I recounted earlier how I spent an entire day in ceaseless prayer for Jayden, spurred by a prophetic dream. For eight relentless hours, I groaned, shedding tears for her soul and crying out to God. Now fast forward three months from that agonizing day, standing in the *kairos* harvest born from those *chronos* prayers.

Throughout the tumultuous journey of ups and downs in the PICU, it seemed as if I could only utter two words, but they resonated with such power that they pierced the darkness: "Jesus reigns."

On one critical night, I reached out to my closest family and friends, urging them to lock onto Jayden's pulse and blood pressure in prayer. A dear friend from across the globe in Australia sent me a voice message. It was 3:00 a.m. on the East Coast in the US, but in Australia, it was 5:00 p.m., day turning into evening. This was a testament to the power of prayer and the God who transcends both *chronos* time and the physical barriers of distance; His time is *kairos*.

While Jayden was in the hospital, her pulse would often dip during the night, but that particular night, it plummeted dangerously low, as if the grip of death had tightened once more. However, the prayers of God's people knocked louder and more persistently than death ever could, echoing the principles of Luke 11:9–10. Like any mother keeping watch for her child, I adamantly refused to surrender to sleep.

The hospital staff pleaded with me, "Mama, you need your rest. We won't leave her side." Then, the Holy Spirit's voice resonated within me: "You can rest!" He gently reminded me that my dear friend in Australia was praying while I slept. Somehow, I dozed off amid the relentless beeping of machines and the blaring pulse alarms.

That's when the dream came. In this vivid dream, three nurses swooped into the PICU room, fervently praying in the Spirit while attending to my daughter. Their voices rang with joy, laughter, and songs of worship. They seamlessly blended worship, prayer, and jubilation. I leaped from the sofa and embraced one of the nurses, exclaiming, "I'm so relieved to know that believers who are also healers are with me, and you pray in tongues!"

But suddenly, I gasped, awakening abruptly. I stood at attention, like a warrior at her post, as the night nurse entered the room. Without missing a beat, I hurried to Jayden's bedside, meeting the nurse halfway. She looked at me and smiled, saying, "You're a great mama. My name is Sydney." Our eyes met, and I smiled back, tears glistening. I knew the Lord had dispatched His Word to heal.

And then it happened: Jayden's pulse plummeted, blood pressure crashed, fingers paled, and body betrayed her as her bowels failed. These were the harbingers of death. Sepsis had returned with a vengeance. The night doctor in the PICU was preoccupied with what appeared to be a more hopeful case, as if he had given up on Jayden. But Sydney and another nurse stood resolute, disdainful of the doctor's seeming resignation. They took charge, ensuring Jayden's comfort and cleanliness and battling the relentless infection. As I assisted in caring for my thirteen-year-old daughter, the nurse asked, "Do you have a medical background?"

"Not officially," I replied. "I'm a minister."

Then, I began to share my story. As the words spilled from my lips, the hair on our arms stood on end. The oppressive spirit of death fled the room. Suddenly, I heard the Lord's voice, whispering, "And they overcame him by the blood of the Lamb, and by the word of their testimony; and they loved not their lives unto death" (Revelation 12:11 KJV). The battle wasn't over in that instant, but darkness knew its time was up. By standing in the gap with Him, by leaning into the Spirit's groans, we had ushered in the promise of resurrection life.

The Bible reminds us that the Spirit Himself intercedes on our behalf with unspoken groanings (Romans 8:26). This way of life, dwelling in the intersection of suffering and glory, involves waiting on Him with unwavering determination and resolutely resisting the enemy's relentless advances. It's a vital understanding, especially when the promise remains concealed, but it's within that gap, in the very space between, that you often find yourself riding on the history you've forged with God. This is the profound essence of reaping history with God.

The Groan for Glory and Reaping History with God

The concept of groaning for glory isn't a purely intellectual endeavor. It's a supernatural transformation that gradually takes shape in the hidden chambers of your heart, forged through trials and tribulations, where words often prove insufficient. Think of Hannah, who wept and longed for a son even before she had the words to express that he would become a priest and a Nazirite. Consider King David, whose yearning to build a dwelling place for God among men originated from a profound, innate groan for the Messiah, etched into his very human essence. And so, in our own lives, we bear the burdens of the Lord, embodying intercession even when we can't fathom the larger design at play.

In a time when it may seem like much is withering away, and many have lost faith in the church, the formation of faithful witnesses has quietly been taking place. Remember the second stage of the witness I spoke about? It's about developing a history with God, crafting a testimony that isn't hearsay but deeply personal. In many ways, my experience with Jayden's miraculous healing was a prophetic picture of what God is doing to resurrect His Church. When the religious system seems to be imploding, and the experts have given up, the Lord is sending faithful witnesses into His Church. They carry with them a history with God, boldly declaring their testimonies, undeterred by rejection. Within the Church, there are those who, like nurse Sydney, have the remarkable ability to unearth these potent testimonies, serving as a reminder to the Church of its true identity in Christ. These are the voices that, with a deep yearning for His glory, bring healing to situations that appear incurable and reconstruct them with life-giving truth.

Friend, here you are, part of this unfolding story. My daughter, Jayden, belongs to Generation Z, and as you read this, you are connected to this narrative. When I cried out for her, I didn't just cry for one child; I unknowingly stepped into a prophetic travail, akin to Hannah's, where I wept not only for her but for her entire generation and the Church of this age. It's a travail that extends to you, the burdened messenger, pulling heaven's power into the earthly realm, and crying out for the strategy of God in this hour.

The countless tears of intercession that I shed for my daughters to become burning messengers of the end times are now intertwined with your own journey. I laid my hands on them daily, even when they were annoyed by my intercessions. These prayers, aimed at releasing His glory and bringing healing to their generation, had long ascended to the throne room of heaven before we found ourselves in this place, yearning for their fulfillment.

In the daily battle, the Lord taught me to quickly reject the accuser's relentless lies. My faith became an unwavering anchor, much like an oak tree rooted in His righteousness. I had not leaned on my own strength for many years, and in the midst of our trials, the unseen realm became more tangible to me than the visible one. I stood shoulder to shoulder with the Lord, watching as the enemy attempted to deceive, much like the fake news in a social media feed. But like a holy spam blocker, the Spirit of God within me cast it away, reminding me that as a messenger and intercessor, I have the power to combat the deceit and bring forth truth.

Could Jayden's healing be a prophetic precursor of an impending awakening? As you journey through this narrative, recognize that you are a messenger of the Lord, an intercessor in the heart of this awakening. Remind yourself of your own history with God in prayer and the promises you've held close.

When I declared my testimony in that hospital room, it felt like a sudden shift in the wind's direction. God's glory crashed upon us like a tidal wave, and the grip of death was shattered. In that moment, the words of Revelation 12:11 resounded in my soul: "They overcame him because of the blood of the Lamb and because of the word of their testimony."

The truth is, all across the earth, there are hidden, holy, unsatisfied sons and daughters crying out for an awakening. Their wordless prayers have risen like incense, beseeching the bride to prepare herself for the Lord's imminent return.

The spirit of the age has tried to wear her down and silence her, but these relentless intercessors, like you, will not cease in their cries on her behalf.

We wrestled with that spirit of death, standing unwavering and intensifying our prayers for the next twelve hours. Finally, after those silent but intense twelve hours, Jayden sat up and humorously shouted to her dad, "Hey, Daddy-o, I gotta pee-o," the way a thirteen-year-old who'd been held hostage without food, water, or a bathroom for days might. We all shared a hearty laugh, and it felt like a celebration was in order. "Get the girl some pizza and a movie, and let her use the bathroom!"

Her liver and kidneys were fully healed, and she came off oxygen after just twenty-four hours, but extensive tests still awaited her. As her blood work continued to improve, the medical staff was baffled and cautiously hopeful, preparing us for a long road of therapy and recovery.

After Jayden's miraculous healing, I found myself in a state of awe. I had witnessed my child journey through the stages of death and then awaken one day fully restored, sporting a new heart, kidneys, liver, and lungs. It was a holy experience, and I realized that I had done nothing but simply exist through it, riding the wave of history with God.

Genuine faithful witnesses are shaped by personal and experiential history with God. We have come to know that He is the embodiment of truth, and every other spirit is a deceiver. This knowledge leads to a profound dissatisfaction with shallow, ankle-deep experiences, as we yearn for the deeper waters. The good news is that these lamenting messengers are the bearers of awakening. The muzzle is being lifted from the mouths of true prophets who have travailed for the revival of His ailing church, much like a mother travails for her child. Can you see yourself in this calling?

The groan for glory is beyond words, and one day, you'll realize that you carry a divine mark you never knew existed. You'll face life-altering tests, and in those moments, you'll do nothing but abide and acknowledge the authenticity of your faith. Like the Shulamite woman, your zealous love becomes more powerful than the grave, and, like David, you'll have a single, deeply etched desire in your DNA. Yet, it may not seem that you're doing anything drastically different from your typical day. You will embody an unspeakable glory that transcends what your eyes see and your ears hear.

Beloved, be prepared, for you will navigate trials differently once you realize that the groan for glory has become an integral part of your perishable body and soul. For instance, when my daughter experienced a creative miracle, I anticipated a joyous celebration, where people would hear her story and receive healing and encouragement. While this did occur in many places, it did not happen where I had expected it.

As the bride begins to come alive once more, many will rejoice, but others will take offense at her newfound freedom and vibrancy. Just as when Jesus raised Lazarus, it stirred the Pharisees to even greater opposition—they not only sought to eliminate Jesus but Lazarus as well.

> When the large crowd of the Jews learned that Jesus was there, they came, not only on account of him but also to see Lazarus, whom he had raised from the dead. So the chief priests made plans to put Lazarus to death as well, because on account of him many of the Jews were going away and believing in Jesus.
>
> —John 12:9–11 ESV

The religious spirit, the Jezebel spirit, or the accusing spirit may persist until Jesus returns. Therefore, we must prepare our hearts. Revival, the awakening we are seeking, can be messy, for the enemy despises the raw power, fire, and glory that it brings. Not everyone will share in our joy, but there is one who always will. He raises a standard against the enemy, and all we must do is remain humble and steadfast in Him. Remember, we have history with Him and declare over every dead thing, "Jesus reigns!"

LET'S ENCOUNTER

In the stillness of your heart, seek to discern the very groan of God, the holy cry that unleashes the power to resurrect the dead and turn a generation back to Him. Allow His peace to wash over you as you close your eyes and wait in silence. Remember, this *chronos* prayer will be harvested in perfect *kairos*.

In this moment, recognize the promises laid before you and acknowledge the brokenness in this world. Embrace the tension between the two. It is within this space that you hold access to His unparalleled power and authority.

Now, as you stand in His presence, ask Him to reveal His tears. Does a face, a family, or a situation come to mind? Can you sense His invitation for you to persist with unwavering intercession, reaching for the prize of His presence? It is from the depths of compassion that resurrection power emerges.

Allow your tears to flow freely, and let the groan within you surface. And in this moment, release your voice to speak life, to speak healing, and to proclaim His promises. Remember your history with God. You are being developed into a faithful witness, a vessel of His glory and power.

PRAY WITH ME

Father, I acknowledge your eternality and that you are not subject to time, and I've been molded to collaborate with you in prayer, transcending my comprehension of time. I recognize that I've been constructing an altar with you along my life's path and in my moments of intercession. Awaken my soul to the profound understanding of your role as the Master of time and the Collector of prayers. Supernaturally increase my trust in you and empower my faith to declare the truth, even when I'm faced with the most daunting challenges. Amen.

5

TIPPING HEAVENLY BOWLS

And when he had taken it, the four living creatures and the
twenty-four elders fell down before the Lamb. Each one had
a harp and they were holding golden bowls full of incense,
which are the prayers of God's people.

—Revelation 5:8 NIV

In the fascinating symphony of intercession, our prayers intertwine with those of the past and rise like incense, filling
the heavenly bowls with the fragrant offerings of our hearts
(Psalm 56:8). At this aroma, the heart of God beats wildly.
Our trust and faith in God are tantalizing to Him. He passionately stores our tears in a bottle and cherishes each cry
and declaration until the appointed time comes and the bowls
of prayer and incense are full (Revelation 5:8). And as the
heavenly bowls fill to overflowing, they tip in response to
God's *kairos* timing, unleashing a flood of holy power and
fulfillment on earth, much like a welcome rain after a long
drought. Often, before the bowl tips, we feel deep anguish of

the soul, and thoughts of doubt try to rob us of our steadfast faith. We stand firm and trust that He is near, and the tipping point is at hand. He is stretching our capacity to withstand greater levels of His glory and power.

Casting Our Crowns

Before the bowls of prayer tip in Revelation chapter 5, we witness the heavenly angelic hosts and elders, utterly mesmerized by the radiant beauty of Jesus, singing, bowing down, and casting their crowns at His feet. One day, we will stand in the presence of Jesus, gazing upon Him as the Lamb who was slain as the ultimate sacrifice, reigning from the center of the throne. As His radiant glory and unmatched beauty shock us, we'll fall on our knees, embracing the wordless truth that our heavenly rewards were not the result of our own efforts but His sacrifice. In that moment of His resplendent majesty, we will realize He used our weak prayers to change history, then we will cast our crowns at His feet, boldly proclaiming that worth, glory, and honor belong solely to Him.

Revelation 4:10–11 (NIV): "The twenty-four elders fall down before him who sits on the throne and worship him who lives forever and ever. They lay their crowns before the throne and say:

'You are worthy, our Lord and God,
    to receive glory and honor and power,
for you created all things,
    and by your will they were created
    and have their being.'"

Can we fathom recognizing His value in this age as we seek Him for His glory to cover the earth? Can we willingly bow low, be stretched further, deepen our surrender, and usher in the full revelation of His glorious value as a life laid down?

In my own journey, I voluntarily set aside my public ministry for a hidden season, primarily within the intimate confines of a prayer room. This period demanded substantial growth. Even when I believed the crucible of testing had ended, the absence of sustainable glory in prayer meetings ignited a deeper longing within me for Him to have His bride, and His reward. What I initially perceived as wasting away in a dim room was, in reality, a profound internal transformation. I cultivated an insatiable hunger and forged a deep connection with God that would fortify me when tragedy struck our family, rendering me unshakable.

God is equipping those who carry His glory to endure higher levels of His presence. Going through phases of surrender and laying everything down expands your capacity to hold more of His presence. The depth of a powerful worship service will leave you yearning, as your personal time with God becomes increasingly fulfilling. Corey Russell says it this way: "The wilderness is the furnace of transformation. It's the context by which God causes all the dross, all the culture, and all its stuff to surface. We get delivered from the masks and the illusions, and we begin to see correctly."[1]

Tarrying unto the Tipping Point

We want the glory without the trials, but the present sufferings cause us to get a vision for what should be. The pressure of the test makes us spiritually violent so that we say to the enemy, "You lose." Before we went through the trial with Jayden, I thought divine healing was great. I prayed for healings, had seen some, and thought we needed to see more. I preached on the demonstration of signs, wonders, and miracles but nicely balanced my message with "We don't chase after these things. They should chase after us." This scriptural statement pointed people to prayer and not pride, which preaches well in a mixed crowd of older saints and zealous youth. Maybe I was a little too nice, as one of my mentors often tells me. He knew I had a fire within me, but I was taming it a little to help people swallow the flaming meat I served up.

I was a preacher with a bit of religion and fear of man. I had never walked in the shoes of a parent who would surely lose their child if God didn't break in. I had not experienced the groan, compassion, and anguish for the promise of healing to manifest as a mother would for her child. I preached about chasing after the face of God but had a little false humility when it came to eagerly desiring the gifts, as if desiring the gifts were in some way arrogant or would cause people to fall away from intimacy with God. (See 1 Corinthians 14:1–5.) Let me say this clearly: It is a religious lie to call watering down the power of God *balancing the message*. The unspoken intercession of the Holy Spirit within you longs for the fullness of His glory. He accomplishes His will, preceding His return, through His spiritually gifted Church. If you want to see bowls of prayer tip, then your prayer life should be white-hot, calling forth the promises of Scripture.

> I consider that our present sufferings are not comparable to the glory that will be revealed in us. *The creation waits in eager expectation for the revelation of the sons of God.* For the creation was subjected to futility, not by its own will, but because of the One who subjected it, *in hope that the creation itself will be set free from its bondage to decay and brought into the glorious freedom of the children of God.*
>
> We know that the whole creation has been groaning together in the pains of childbirth until the present time. Not

only that, but we ourselves, who have the first fruits of the Spirit, groan inwardly as we wait eagerly for our adoption as sons, the redemption of our bodies.

—Romans 8:18–23 BSB, emphasis added

Notice my emphasis above: *"The creation waits in eager expectation for the revelation of the sons of God . . . in hope that the creation itself will be set free from its bondage to decay and brought into the glorious freedom of the children of God."* Creation is groaning for the children of God to be unveiled and take their rightful place. The hope is in Jesus, in His coming, and in the day when pain, suffering, and tears will be no more. Beloved, you and I have a massive part to play in the hope of all creation. Pray for His fullness and declare His truth.

Jesus prayed to the Father concerning the disciples: "The glory which you have given Me I also have given to them" (John 17:22). Are we truly sons if we solely seek His glory but reject the gifts, callings, and power necessary to reveal Him on earth? When death knocked at our door, we needed heaven's bowls to be poured out without concern for the opinions of others regarding our words, actions, or heavenly petitions. We were not playing religious games.

Spiritual Violence, Earthly Peace

They asked me, "Mama, do you understand? She is critical. We are sending you our chaplain. Let me say this clearly: Your daughter may not make it. She's a very sick girl."

She had arrived at the PICU on life support in their most urgent ambulance. Not one doctor but teams of specialists met us at the door. They swarmed around my girl and pulled me aside as everything was moving in slow motion around me. I felt compelled to do two things—keep my hand on her and pray in the Spirit.

Have you ever been there? It's as if people are talking to you in a foreign language; you see their mouths moving, but words aren't computing. You don't know if you are being strong or losing your mind. Most people panic; I was eerily calm. I had the "peace that surpasses all understanding" guarding my heart and mind, but to the medical staff, I seemed to be in denial. My response was steadfast as I maintained firm faith and bold prayers for 90 percent of the eight days we spent in PICU.

The most tender place in your heart is your children, and you will go into hell itself to rip the face off an enemy. You won't think twice about dying to protect them. But can you *be still internally* when the enemy hurls his violent lies at you and accuses you of their pain?

As a burning messenger, one area that will make you the most spiritually violent is your family. Still, it's also your weakest area for anxiety and fear-driven reactions. During this time, I sat at another level of the desert while the accuser raged. Anxiety and fear are opposing forces to faith, hope, and love. Satan wants us to fall apart. He drives us to be reactionary— shifting blame to one another, God, and yes, even to him.

When you have a groan in you for the fullness of the kingdom, you will experience the enemy's low blows, but you must remember your war is not against flesh and blood. Every little moment of pressure is an opportunity to strengthen reliance on the Lord. You'd better know who you are, know the voice of your Father, and aim your roar in the right place if you are going to run the fiery race for the long haul. "From the days of John the Baptist until now the kingdom of heaven has suffered violence, and the violent take it by force" (Matthew 11:12 ESV).

Embrace spiritual boldness in your prayers, demanding the unwavering manifestation of God's Word and the utter dismantling of the enemy's schemes. Be relentless in your pursuit of the fullness of His kingdom, while remaining a harbinger of peace and love towards those who accuse you. Let your life be a testament to your unwavering faith and commitment to God's will while laying down your rights to win carnal arguments.

Maranatha

A deep, visceral longing for the coming of the Lord had stirred within my soul long before I found myself in need of a divine miracle. My tears of intercession, like fragrant incense, have soaked altars, bedrooms, and living rooms as I cried out for the glory to descend upon the Church and Generation Z.

This groan is also within you, panting in harmony with the longing of all creation for Jesus's return. Maranatha, "Come, Lord Jesus," is more than a mere expression; it is woven into the profound groan spoken of in Romans 8:26. In this unity between the Holy Spirit and the spirit of the bride, there resounds a cry for His magnitude and return.

When we engage in wordless intercession, we find ourselves in sync with the Spirit's deep yearning for the fullness of God to manifest. As we navigate our brief existence on this side of eternity, we must be gripped by the words of John 9:4, which compel us to diligently carry out the work of Him who sent us while the daylight remains, thus intensifying our intercession for the glorious presence and power of God to flood the earth.

As the day of the Lord draws near, you and I have a mission: "While it is daytime, we must do the works of Him who sent Me. Night is coming, when no one can work" (John 9:4 BSB).

In the face of mounting intensity, many will bury their heads in the sand, attempting to stifle the voices that proclaim and demonstrate the kingdom of heaven. Yet, those who are sent will arrive, bearing signs, wonders, and miracles illuminating His kingdom and His reign. Some with hardened hearts will seek to silence these wild intercessions, testimonies, and declarations.

However, I prophesy that pioneering mothers and fathers will pass their mantles to the emerging voices, empowering them, much like the Bridegroom empowers His bride. Those who carry the weight of the maranatha groan understand that without the next generation walking in increased authority, power, revelation of Jesus, and the force of prayer, spiritual decay is inevitable.

Weighty Glory as the Generations Run Together

The generations must align, each one paving the path for the next. Deep within, there's a shared understanding that one of these generations will be the one that ushers in the Lord's return. A new John the Baptist generation has arisen, carrying the language for the wordless prayers of the preceding generation after being forged in the crucible of the wilderness. They turn away from the accolades of men, choosing the wilderness because their cry transcends the confines of performance-centered church systems, and their call resounds: "He's coming. Repent, for the day of the Lord is near."

Are these the ones who sound the final alarm before Jesus's showdown and millennial reign? I cannot say, but the impending visitation of the Lord holds more weight than we can fathom. As the generations run in harmony, monumental glory will descend.

Understand that an intercessor and true messenger of the Lord never retires. Once His intercessions have seized you, they grip you for life. Yet remember that these groans, travails, and tears serve a purpose.

Hearts Returning and Realigning

As we anticipate the tipping of heaven's prayer bowls, one significant aspect lies in the supernatural reconnection of the hearts of the sons with the fathers. This reconnection isn't just about family or ministry ties but also concerns the restoration of ancient pathways and the revelation of eternal truths, aligning our hearts with the wisdom of the early fathers of the faith and the eternal ways of God.

Malachi 4:5–6 says Elijah would arouse holy fire and cause the faithful generation to long for the rebellious sons. Ministers often prophetically quote this passage to respect and reconcile younger and elder saints. Most who carry the heart of the Lord are provoked to tears by the younger generation's disjointedness and immorality, and the power of this passage is a comforting promise we should do war with. But when we solely apply prophetic Scriptures to our present day, we may limit our understanding. There is more being unveiled here for us than meets the eye. Consider intercession and Malachi's end-of-the-age prophecy:

> Behold, I am going to send you Elijah the prophet before the coming of the great and terrible day of the LORD. He will turn the hearts of the fathers back to their children and the hearts of the children to their fathers, so that I will not come and strike the land with complete destruction.
>
> —Malachi 4:5–6

The rallying cry is for the fathers' hearts to be turned to the sons, and the sons' hearts to the fathers'—so that the Father might not smite our land in judgment. Intercession and revelation are interior acts of reconciliation in which our hearts turn to individuals whom our minds believe are hopeless. John the Baptist appeared in the spirit and might of Elijah. He paved the way for Jesus to be revealed as the one who would reconcile mankind to the Father. Our fervent prayer is for our children and grandchildren to rise with holy boldness and prepare the way of the Lord. With each passing century, the demand for mankind's restoration to the Father grows louder. Our prayers are joined by those of others who have fought this battle of faith before us.

Meanwhile, the unfinished intercessions of those in Hebrews 11 and 12, the martyrs, the unjustly killed, and the great cloud of witnesses, are still at work gripping you and me for the fullness of reconciliation. We may not have words for it, but our spirits yearn for our Father's ancient paths, for His original design for humanity, and for the return of His wayward children to Himself. Our prayers are more powerful than we realize when we cry out for the current children to return to the ways of old. We unite with ancient prayers; we cry out for generations ahead to walk in the ways of the Lord. We are committing to disciple the young and ignite elders' zeal by honoring their wisdom. In this, hearts return to one another, and we simultaneously prepare for the Lord's return. In a sense, we join with the intercessions of John the Baptist in the spirit of Elijah.

As we run together in the fear of the Lord and obedience to His Spirit, the bowls of intercession for awakening will begin to tip. The glory will be so heavy that pastors will be unable to conduct church as usual. This movement's hallmark will be intercession. No one will preach until they are confident that they hold the words of life. This marks the inception of our hearts returning to the ancient pathways. With the spirit of Elijah resting upon a new generation, Jesus takes His rightful place as the honored leader of His Church, and His messengers are embraced as lovesick intercessors.

He's More than the God of Conferences

Let this be a firm warning: The measurement of our personal maturity in Christ should never be solely based on the level of manifestations we witness in conferences or meetings. Allow me to introduce you to someone who understands this truth. I encountered Andrew in the Middle East among underground church leaders. He endured two years of imprisonment in Turkey for his faith, fervently crying out to God for a divine encounter. In the years prior, powerful manifestations of God's presence had sustained him during revival conferences in the challenging Turkish mission field. However, to his dismay, his time in prison was marked by an agonizing silence from the Lord, revealing that the fullness of God transcends mere manifestations.

> When I was in prison, I experienced the total silence of God. I was really shocked by it. I did not have a sense of God's presence throughout my time in prison, and after this had been my main value—what I ran after for years—I felt like, *you've abandoned me. How could you do this to your son?*. . . I said, *Are you just a God of conferences?* Where are you in my darkest time when I really need your presence?[2]

Andrew later recounted his wife's remarkable peace during her own imprisonment, underscoring her years of sitting alone with the Lord in deep intercession. Could it be that the inner world of an intercessor holds more significance than a corporate gathering than we've ever recognized? While I've witnessed the majestic presence of God leave a room stunned during corporate services, Andrew's experience sheds light on the fleeting nature of these moments, especially in the cold isolation of a prison cell.

It's often been said by leaders like Lou Engle in the prayer movement that we have not yet truly experienced the spirit of prayer. Initially, I questioned this statement, believing we had already experienced profound intercession together in the prayer room. But what if the dissatisfaction of these older leaders stems from the longing within their private prayer life? What if we shift our focus away from the clamor of grandiose gatherings and instead center our efforts on cultivating profound intimacy with God in the silence? Could this potentially unlock unprecedented levels of intercession when we come together, with the worship teams and extravagance? Can Andrew's words, like those of leaders like Lou, speak about more power in prayer and be a wake-up call to inspire us to go deeper?

Lou's hunger for more brings to mind King David's longing to build a dwelling place for God, but instead, the Lord built David's house, his lineage, to be a perpetual host for Him (1 Chronicles 22:8, 28:3; 2 Samuel 7:12–16; Luke 1:31–33). In the prayer room, there were moments when I felt like a sobbing misfit, my hunger for the fullness of God burning within me. Perhaps I'm connecting with the intercessions of leaders like Lou and others, for, as they've rightly put it, there's more.

When we're alone in the secret place, where our tears have their own language and we cry out for more without knowing exactly what we want, we are drawn into an intimate experience with God. When we come together, whether in a crowded gathering or in solitude, the atmosphere changes. Microphones drop, knees bend like wax, faces touch the floor, and tears flow silently. In this sacred space, you can hear it all: audible groans, weeping, wailing, laughter, spontaneous declarations, and prophetic songs. Then, as suddenly as it began, silence descends upon the room.

I've encountered this atmosphere both in a crowded setting and when I'm alone with God. He desires that we experience His presence just as intensely when we gather as we do alone. The interior life of prayer acts as a lightning rod, drawing His presence for others to encounter. When we gather, bringing the depth of our personal intercession, a convergence of power occurs as each of us brings facets of His glory. Hiddenness fosters a hunger for God alone, authenticity, and humility in the fractured, imperfect vessels He chooses to use.

I often ponder what Lou Engle and other prayer movement pioneers have encountered in their intimate moments with God, prompting them to declare, "We have not yet arrived!" Their tears and travails have surely filled heavenly bowls, petitioning for the unexplainable. Now I comprehend that I was not a misfit, but a torchbearer of travail, yearning for Jesus to receive His full reward. Perhaps this emerging generation is destined to manifest the glory that pioneers like Heidi Baker, Bill Johnson, Cindy Jacobs, Randy Clark, Lou Engle, and others longed to witness, for they birthed us in moments of desperate intercession.

Could it be that those of us in our thirties to fifties are called to consecrate ourselves once more, joining hands to transform their tears into a sustained outpouring of fire and glory? Solomon, David's son, bore witness to the power of his father's prayers. In Psalm 132, the writer implores God to remember David and the inner battles he fought. He reminds God of David's resolve to build a dwelling place and the promise that the Messiah would descend from David's lineage. David's vision of God's presence dwelling in Israel was ultimately realized through Solomon.

> Now all the priests who were present had consecrated themselves regardless of their divisions. And when the priests came

out of the Holy Place, all the Levitical singers—Asaph, Heman, Jeduthun, and their sons and relatives—stood on the east side of the altar, dressed in fine linen and playing cymbals, harps, and lyres, accompanied by 120 priests sounding trumpets. The trumpeters and singers joined together to praise and thank the LORD with one voice. They lifted up their voices, accompanied by trumpets, cymbals, and musical instruments, in praise to the LORD:

"For He is good;
   His loving devotion endures forever."

And the temple, the house of the LORD, was filled with a cloud so that the priests could not stand there to minister because of the cloud; for the glory of the LORD filled the house of God.

—2 Chronicles 5:11–14 BSB

Shockingly, Scripture makes it clear that Solomon experienced the manifestation of his father's prayers. God worked through the son but faithfully fulfilled the petitions of David. This is the purest essence of glory—the manifestation of the fear of the Lord. Those who once took pride in their toil and sacrifices now humbly acknowledge, "The true builder and architect is the Lord."

When the hearts of mothers and fathers ache for their sons and daughters, when their yearning transcends words and ascends to spiritual realms, a profound transformation occurs. Their silent cries become a clarion call to the next generation, sparking a spiritual quickening. I remember a time when I, wounded and estranged from my family and the Lord, experienced the depth of my own mother's intercession. With tear-filled eyes, she groaned in prayer, pleading, "God, rip her from the clutches of Satan." Remarkably, the very next morning, I awoke with an unquenchable longing for God.

Years later, as a parent, I echoed my mother's prayers. "God, release her and her generation from the grip of Satan." My mother and I could never have foreseen the profound impact our wordless gasps and tear-soaked pleas would have. She yearned for my return, but God's plan exceeded even her wildest imagination.

The cries of a generation resonate for the next. My plea for my child can also be translated akin to Hannah's: "God, turn the hearts of this generation back to you. Give us this generation, and we will consecrate them to you."

Solomon's ability to construct the majestic temple was an outcome of David's cries. This place of glory became a place of unparalleled splendor, where the nation communed with God. In retrospect, we must all realize that we are not the sole builders; rather, we were merely the recipients of someone else's intercessions. Construction unfolds precisely when the Lord tips the bowls of intercession, instantly releasing provision, resources, builders, glory, and holy fire for the endeavor.

And when He shows up, a cry breaks forth from deep within, resonating in every heart, proclaiming, "You, Lord, are worthy above all others." He longs to do in our day what He accomplished in the times of Solomon, Elijah, and those who waited for Him in the upper room. Sons and daughters are called to prophesy and implement strategies born from visions, while pioneering mothers and fathers must entrust their dreams and prayers are gripping the coming generation of builders. David yearned to construct God a house, but he pioneered with a tent and a dream. Similarly, many mothers and fathers have aspirations to construct new wineskin churches, but God's calling often extends to building people more than buildings. Through your journey of travailing with Him, you now hold the keys to unlock the heavenly structures.

The Lord invites you to come alongside those with divine blueprints in commencing construction while remind them to cherish the hidden place of prayer. The blueprints they possess are wineskins that reflect heaven's design. Help them consecrate themselves anew, and equip them with the tools you've preserved for this very moment.

The Culmination and Your Role in the Eternal Narrative

As you've contemplated the tipping of the heavenly bowls in your personal prayers and witnessed the collective prayers of those who've gone before you being poured out for awakening and healing, it is imperative to grasp the profound personal significance within the broader eschatological context. These moments, where your heartfelt petitions align with prophetic prayers of the past, serve as a microcosm of the grand narrative. The tipping of heaven's golden bowls mirrors the fulfillment of God's divine plan, heralding the imminent return of the Lord and the culmination of end-times events.

Your prayers and the collective intercession spanning generations are woven into the tapestry of the eternal storyline, creating a deep and personal connection with the overarching narrative of God's redemptive history. In this pivotal hour, you are summoned to bear the torch of prayer and ministry, for your unwavering intercession possesses the transformative power to shape the destinies of nations and to usher in the eternal purposes of God.

LET'S ENCOUNTER

I prophesy to you: Heaven's bowls are rapidly filling, not just with your fervent prayers but with the cries of those who were gripped by God before your time. He's orchestrating reconcilia-tion, turning the hearts of the younger generation back to their forefathers, and these promises will be fulfilled as your prayers begin to tip the golden bowls of incense. He will reveal Himself in unprecedented ways before His return, in line with His grand plan that weaves into His specific purpose for you and those you intercede for. Cry out for Him to kindle within you an insatiable hunger, an unquenchable thirst, and a deep groaning.

Remember David, in unshakable faith, rested assured that he would indeed "see the goodness of the LORD in the land of the living" (Psalm 27:13 NIV). He diligently prepared his son and his kingdom for the same. Likewise, you are called to prepare yourself, your family, and your church to embrace a lifestyle steeped in prayer and fasting. Just as David's faith never wavered, you too can trust that when God speaks, He faithfully fulfills His promises. With unshakable confidence, respond to God, affirming that your prayers have been heard, believing that they are seamlessly interwoven with the prayers of countless others, filling the heavenly bowls to the brim.

PRAY WITH ME

Jesus, I refuse to settle. Open my spiritual eyes to comprehend intercession, your timing, and the bowls of prayer in heaven. Grip my heart with longing for the younger and older gen-erations to return to you that you would be glorified. I also ask that you would personally confirm this new revelation to me. Give me boldness to pray for the sick, for revival, and for your glory to fill the room where I sit. I want to see you demonstrate the power of the Gospel in my life and in my family. Amen.

6

THE UNSEEN WAR

Remember, Satan fears virtue. He is terrified of humility; he hates it because humility is the surrender of the soul to the Lord, and the devil is terrified of Jesus Christ.

—Francis Frangipane

When the Spirit seizes you, your human spirit quickens. It's like a newborn's first breath outside the womb. The Spirit, God's very breath, stirs within you as you cry out, "Abba, Father," announcing to the hosts of heaven your spiritual rebirth. You become one surrendered to the Lamb of God, an adversary of the devil, a witness, and in this, you are crucified with Christ yet eternally alive (Romans 8:17).

By this you know the Spirit of God: every spirit that confesses that Jesus Christ has come in the flesh is from God; and every spirit that does not confess Jesus is not from God; this is the

spirit of the antichrist, which you have heard is coming, and
now it is already in the world.

—1 John 4:2–3

The witness of the Spirit residing within you boldly testifies
that Jesus Christ is the Messiah and affirms your identity as
a child of God. It resounds with the proclamation that you've
enlisted in the army of the Lord. From this point onward, your
very core discerns what aligns with Christ and what opposes
Him. If someone claims to be Christ, they are influenced by a
contrary spirit, and any ideology that opposes Christ embodies the spirit of the antichrist. To clarify further, the antichrist
spirit seeks to draw us away from embracing our status as
adopted sons and daughters of God. As we delve into the
profound spiritual transformation that occurs through different forms of wordless prayer, we gain insight into the Spirit's
role in shaping us into faithful witnesses in an increasingly
antichrist culture.

The Holy Spirit intervenes to renew your mind, will, and
emotions, equipping you to clearly distinguish His guidance
from the allure of worldly desires and the spiritual opposition
that undermines Christ's kingdom. In this critical hour, it's
imperative to cultivate a deep love for God's truth and main-
tain daily communion with His Spirit. Your prayer should
echo, "Lord, sharpen my discernment and ignite a passion
for the truth," for the Holy Spirit bears witness to the truth,
while every other spirit is a deceiver (see 2 Thessalonians
2:9–12).

As an heir of Christ, you rely on His witness not only to
discern the truth but also to unmask the devil's deceit. This
is no ordinary battle; it's an invisible spiritual warfare. It is
essential for you, as an intercessor and messenger of God, to
cultivate a firm biblical understanding of this hidden conflict

and equip yourself for peace and strategic prayer, enabling you to function effectively as an intercessor, a parent, a son or daughter, and a herald of the end times.

As Francis Frangipane wisely pointed out, the devil is deeply threatened by humility because it serves as a testament to a life fully surrendered to Christ. Humility acknowledges that our battle is not against mere flesh and blood yet won through the cross of Christ (Ephesians 6:12). The adversary strives to keep us in a state of turmoil, provoking our fight-or-flight instincts. Yet rather than becoming entangled with or disregarding the demonic forces, we must find authority and clarity by aligning our hearts with Christ, seeking His guidance and peace even in the fiercest storms. The Holy Spirit's inner witness opens doors to revelation knowledge and enables us to discern with precision whom we labor alongside—Jesus the Messiah—and what forces are at play in the world, those of the antichrist spirit. The battle is hidden from plain sight, yet Satan's purpose remains straightforward: to discredit the Messiah and undermine the profound potency of the cross.

Seated and Hidden

In the realm of the spirit, everything functions in obscurity—God, the adversary, the angelic hosts of heaven. The true essence of eternity lies in the unseen, while the temporary is decaying before our eyes. To truly grasp the enigmatic nature of this unseen battle, we must first recognize the inherent power that lies within the realm of hiddenness. When we align ourselves with Him, we walk in victory even in the enemy's turbulent domain. We become a living testament to the unwavering might inherent in Christ, allowing us to rise above the mirage of decay.

The sting of rejection becomes all too real when we choose to live as foreigners in this world. Many times, I've felt profoundly misunderstood, a painful struggle for those who are wholeheartedly devoted to Christ. You open your heart and serve others, and sooner or later, someone takes offense or remains dissatisfied with your care. Yet, this time, it felt as if all hell itself were infiltrating the minds of those I held dear, contorting my character and intentions. The accuser drew nearer, shattering my heart into pieces, urging me to surrender. But I understood that I had to find my way back to the peace of being concealed in Christ. I knew that if I could simply remain still in Him, Jesus would fight on my behalf.

In the midst of this fierce spiritual battle, an overwhelming peace enveloped me. As the demonic forces surrounded me, I closed my eyes, tapping into my position of being seated with Christ. In that moment, a radiant light seemed to emanate from me, dispelling the darkness and scattering the demonic accusations, leaving me with a prayer strategy, hope, peace, and victory. He was fighting for me and with me in intercession, and I would soon experience redemption and reconciliation. When we position ourselves in Him, we stay out of the enemy's chaos zone and become a living testament to the unshakable strength found in Christ so that we can live above the fray.

Yes, you'll endure hardships as you follow Jesus's example of obedience, but the future glory and heavenly authority that await you far surpass any present suffering (see Romans 12:12; Luke 9:23; Hebrews 5:8; Romans 8:18). From this heavenly blood-bought seat, you learn to behold and trust Him and take hold of His unspoken mysteries. From the throne room, war room strategies are unveiled. Here, you will enjoy breathtaking encounters with Him, see what He is doing, hear what He is praying, and become laser-accurate in your prayers and prophetic gifts. Here, your discernment is sharpened and clarified. In this place, you are at peace and covered in Psalm 91 protection. In this place, you discover the overflow of strength to execute His strategies and gain the wisdom to heed no voice or ideology other than that of the King of kings.

Your burden will make sense, and you will carry it yoked to Him. You are a co-laborer with Christ to carry out His heavenly blueprint in the world's darkest hour. Humility serves as the gateway to the profound experience of sitting with Him, aligning with His zealous heart. You must understand that being misunderstood is part of this journey. When you embrace both the humility and the zeal of the Lord for His bride, know that He is faithful to bring these to fruition to secure your victory in this unseen war.

The Power of Agreement with God

Just as electrons in a circuit align and flow in agreement to generate electrical power, in prayer, the unity of hearts aligned with God serves as a conduit for the unfolding of God's eternal plan. Scripture affirms that when we align our hearts with God, He answers our prayers, a simple truth that was sufficient for me when I was a new believer. In my childlike faith, no proof was needed, only truth. Discover what God is saying and agree—that's it!

I witnessed astounding miracles, from unexpected healings to bills miraculously paid, and even the gift of a new language to share the Gospel with a Spanish-speaking woman. Simply, I read the Scriptures and acted on them without an ounce of doubt. In the words of Buddy in the Christmas movie *Elf*, I was essentially shouting, "I'm in love! I'm in love! And I don't care who knows it!"[1] Sadly, we will encounter what seems like unanswered prayer and confront skeptical critics; doubt can find its way into the crevices of our faith. We must bear in mind that the battle for our faith unfolds in the unseen realm and necessitates a conscious alignment of our thoughts with God and His Word. Unshakable faith requires a deliberate connection to the profound power of the cross and the reality of eternal life.

When it comes to the realm of power, I understand *agreement* to mean the dynamic fusion of forces, ideas, or individuals uniting with seamless precision to unleash amplified impact toward a shared passion. World-changing agreement with God isn't just nodding in approval during church gatherings, halfheartedly reciting Scripture in moments of difficulty, or shouting "Amen" when others pray, express their struggles, or make requests. While these responses can create moments of connection and encourage us to walk closer with God, they may not always amount to childlike and proactive agreement. As we mature in Christ, we must develop the discipline of clothing our perishable nature with the imperishable and commanding our mortality to take on immortality; we will be challenged by the forces of darkness.

As the apostle Paul says in 1 Corinthians 15:53–55, our minds, wills, emotions, and bodies must submit to the Spirit of God, who is immortal and eternal. In my young whirlwind of faith, I encouraged others to come and pray with me for the sick. On a few occasions, we went to visit critically ill people in hospice. We were riding on the wave of healings seen in the weeks before, and we were ready to take on hard cases because the Scriptures say nothing is too hard for God.

And then it happened: Someone we prayed for died. Heartbroken, we took a step back and asked God why. He answered with Ecclesiastes 3:2, "[There is] a time to be born and a time to die" (NIV). I was sad for the loss and a little confused by why this one died but another was healed. But I was happy to agree with His Word. He was teaching me more about Himself and how to walk according to the Spirit of truth.

You were created to demonstrate the power of the Gospel with wild faith. As Bible teacher and author Arthur Wallis said, "Try to discover what God is doing in your time, and fling yourself into the accomplishment of His purpose and will."[2] You were made to unveil the hidden kingdom of God on earth. This assignment requires you to know what He says and does, especially when His goodness helps you understand His seasons. This hour will challenge us to know His heart and move at the sound of His voice, just as Jesus did. Jesus saw what the Father was doing and did it, heard what the Father was saying and said it, and knew when the Father was telling Him to wait for the greater glory, as with Lazarus; and when it was time for the cross, He pressed into agreement with heaven as well.

Abiding in the Spirit and the Promised Rest

The Lord taught me the concept of spiritual rest the hard way. I'll get to that story in a moment. When we pray from the realm of the Spirit, we align ourselves with His Word; and in Ephesians 6:18 Paul encourages us to "pray in the spirit at all times." We will discuss spiritual language at length in chapter 8. For now we must note that speaking in tongues serves as a means to enter the realm of the Spirit in prayer. Paul's exhortation provides us with the destination from which we pray—praying *in* the Spirit—which leads us in power, love, and truth. This is simpler than you may think, requiring only trust in the Lord and belief in the covenant rest achieved through Jesus's blood.

Ephesians 2:5–6 teaches that we are already seated with God in the place of intercession because of His sacrifice for us.

When we recognize that our prayers are more spiritual than intellectual, the war becomes about resting our souls, trusting, listening, and embracing the spiritual value of the blood of Jesus. Once we grasp the power of being still, acknowledging, and hearing Him, we enter mature spiritual work, rending heaven.

The teachings in Hebrews 3–4 highlight the significance of faith and obedience in abiding in the spiritual realm of peace. The author urges believers to enter into God's rest, emphasizing that it goes beyond our physical state. He makes it clear that the Israelites did not enter promised *shabbat* because of unbelief. In His rest, we lay down our full weight and come to know the faithfulness of our Father and His provision. Here, we are looking to Him for intimacy and wholeness, which is beyond divine direction or power. As we place our trust in God's promises, surrender our worries, and stop striving, we enter a supernatural place of *shalom* that surpasses earthly circumstances. Here, the substance of our faith is formed and nothing is missing or broken.

As I said, the Lord taught me the concept of spiritual shalom the hard way. You may be less determined than me and know how to abide when the Lord says so. I mastered quietness. I learned to cope with stress by unashamedly canceling appointments or turning down opportunities that coincided with my priorities, but spiritual rest is different. The enemy certainly pounces on us in our most vulnerable times, trying to distract and prevent us from achieving true shalom. When our circumstances overwhelm us, we become more vulnerable to succumbing to the attacks.

As you know, the last few weeks of school are stressful for moms and teachers. One Thursday afternoon in May, I was laden with commitments and appointments I had to keep. Our oldest daughter was graduating from high school and going to her senior prom, our middle daughter was graduating from eighth grade, our youngest was performing four dances in her biggest recital of the year, and I had a book deadline, a senior photo shoot, and an enormous family coming to town to celebrate. Can anyone say, "False burden"?

I was overwhelmed and cried out to God, but He was quiet. I stared out the window like a zombie, stuck in time. I wondered whether I could jump in the hot tub and hide underwater. I smiled and told God I needed to get baptized! When my body hit the water, the Lord overwhelmed me with supernatural peace. My phone rang, and the calm lifted. I thought, *I don't have time to be in the hot tub.* I got out, shifted my effort into high gear, and smacked my skull on a shelf corner. *I don't have time . . .* I thought as I fell.

Boom! Everything went black. I awoke to a bleeding head. I hobbled to the freezer, grabbed a bag of frozen green beans, wrapped them in a towel, put them on my head, and called my husband. He advised me to relax. *No way, no time.* I carried on cleaning and preparing until I could no longer. I had a concussion. Did you know that concussions require brain rest? I didn't. Brain rest is complete mental and physical inactivity. Now only one thing mattered: being present. I had to trust Him to handle the schedule, expectations, and overload.

On Friday, our beautiful eldest daughter walked down the stairs in her teal blue prom dress, our miracle girl was honored at graduation, and our baby girl appeared in her jazzy dance costume and ballet bun. The kids and family had fun. The house's flaws didn't matter, and the professional photographer canceled, which was actually a blessing. At 7:00 p.m., when I sat down in the auditorium to watch our baby's dance performance, the Lord spoke: "Inactivity is not rest. It is a coping mechanism. It is time you enter the greater shalom I won for you on the cross. I have a realm of rest available. Shalom means abiding with me in heavenly places, trusting me during storms, and believing that in me nothing is missing or broken."

Inactivity and mental calmness are behavior modification. Faith is not an idea but a substance we access. This substance develops our spiritual eyes to see what is unseen by the carnal eyes in times of stress and uncertainty (Hebrews 11:1). Through faith or trust in the Lord, we can enter the spiritual realm of rest, which lets us confidently approach God's throne of grace and find peace in His presence. In this realm, we experience peace that goes beyond our understanding. Through the substance of faith, we are given the strength to face the challenges of life with unwavering confidence. In this holy realm, our prayers hold authority, aligning with God's will as recorded in the scrolls of heaven, and working to manifest His purposes on earth. When we feel overwhelmed, we simply agree with Him and lay all of our weight down at His feet.

Agreement in faith is vertical and horizontal. Matthew 18:19 captures Jesus's words: "Again I say to you, if two of you agree on earth about anything they ask, it will be done for them by my Father in heaven" (ESV). A powerful synergy is created when our hearts and desires tremble and when we choose to believe God, ask for His plan to be revealed to us, and unite in agreement with other believers. Trust Him in times of personal strain, yes, but call on others to intercede in agreement. Then you will experience the joy of a lovesick community. God longs for us to share one another's burdens and for us to contend together. As we unite in sync with God, we cooperate with Him and see Him at work; this testifies to His faithfulness and catalyzes the fulfillment of His promises. When we passionately embrace His truth and obey His Word, we ignite a holy fire within and align in agreement with the kingdom's grand plan and holy rest.

The Activity of Angels in Prayer

In response to our faith, God dispatches His angels as ministering spirits to accomplish His purposes on earth. Hebrews 1:14 reveals that angels are sent to serve and assist those who belong to Christ. They act as agents of God's will, carrying out tasks and ministering to those who align themselves with His purposes. I have experienced the Lord sending His messengers to help lighten my load. That Thursday in May just before I hit my head, I cried out for God to stop all the chaos and send help. He did not cause me to bust my head, but angels moved when I cried out. He sent helpers to complete the needed work for the day and bring peace to the storm. Psalm 103:20 says that angels obediently fulfill God's commands and are dispatched to defend, heal, and carry out His will for your life. I fully believe angels were dispatched to aid me that day.

As we embrace God's truth and walk in obedience to His Word, we activate a spiritual synergy that attracts angelic intervention. Our faith and their help enable God's perfect plan to be accomplished with power and precision. Angels are drawn when we speak the Word of God and pray. They love to act when we passionately radiate the presence of the Holy Spirit and fervently proclaim the Word of God.

Becoming a Landing Strip

The same way angels move at the sound of the word of God through us, so the enemy's imps move when we accuse, condemn, curse, and complain about God or siblings in Christ. The adversary wants us to blame God and others for his vile wreckage. Unfortunately, we give him our power to play his games. We can choose to become a landing strip either for God or for the devil's devices.

We've discussed how angels move at the word of the Lord, which includes our worship, prayers, conversations, declarations, and such. Let's go back to the Garden to understand the authority we have and how Satan wanted it all along. God granted Adam and Eve dominion over the earth, and they enjoyed unbroken fellowship with Him in the Garden. Nonetheless, in a moment of uncertainty that ultimately led to distrust of God and a self-centered perspective, Adam and Eve handed the dominion to Satan.

Satan accused God of withholding goodness, godlikeness, and knowledge. They fell into his lies and accusations. Satan exploited them so he could use them as a platform for his deceitful schemes. His game is still the same. He does not have his own authority on earth because Christ's suffering cleared the way for us to be restored as intercessors and righteous rulers in God's kingdom. But that does not stop that slithering serpent from whispering lies and accusations in our ears to get a little power back.

When you embody the lifestyle of the cross, you become a landing strip for the kingdom of heaven to manifest and be established on earth in answer to creation's groans and Jesus's prayers.

> And I heard a loud voice in heaven saying: "Now have come the salvation and the power and the kingdom of our God, and the authority of His Christ. For the accuser of our brothers has been thrown down—he who accuses them day and night before our God."
>
> —Revelation 12:10 BSB

Satan has no authority, only twisted power. He needs someone to agree with his distorted accusations to bring charges against God's elect. Jesus expressed to His disciples this mystery when He breathed on them to receive His Spirit: "If you forgive the sins of any, their sins have been forgiven them; if you retain the sins of any, they have been retained" (John 20:23). We have the power to forgive sins through His Spirit.

Jesus's words concerning forgiveness of sins are so powerful. The weight of keeping someone's wrongdoing against them should make us cry when we realize how the accuser uses our testimony against us and them. Satan wants our agreement, but as we forgive and release, the Lamb's blood binds him and releases them. Unfortunately, when we agree with his charges against someone, he enacts consequences on us, them, and our families.

The Bible says, "And when you stand to pray, if you hold anything against another, forgive it, so that your Father in heaven will forgive your trespasses as well" (Mark 11:25 BSB; see also Matthew 6:14; Luke 6:27; Colossians 3:13). In Christ, we are ambassadors on assignment to bring heaven to earth. We must break agreement with the accuser and bless those who curse. Jesus says in 1 Peter 3:9, "Do not repay evil with evil or insult with insult. On the contrary, repay evil with blessing, because to this you were called so that you may inherit a blessing" (NIV). In Matthew 16:19, He says, "I will give you the keys of the kingdom of heaven; whatever you bind on earth will be bound in heaven, and whatever you loose on earth will be loosed in heaven" (NIV). We never want to become a conduit of the enemy's assaults.

One way to help someone find freedom in Christ is to forgive the wrongs they committed and intercede for their salvation. My husband and I have been married for two decades at the time of this writing. It is easy to agree with the enemy that he will never change in certain areas of personality or thinking. But I have watched the Lord move supernaturally in my husband's heart and seen drastic changes happen within

We do not fight with arrows of accusation but with forgiveness and prophetic declaration.

a day of forgiving him and blessing him in prayer.

It's important to approach forgiveness with a pure heart and not hold on to bitterness. In fact, forgiveness is directly tied to overcoming temptation and avoiding evil. By praying for those who have wronged you, even in small areas, and forgiving them, you can break the hold that Satan has on them and help prevent negative consequences from affecting your family. This act of forgiveness can have a powerful impact on your family's history and future. Remember, forgiveness unleashes blessing, and accusation opens the door to cursing.

Satan and his demons are rebels against the kingdom of God. They roam across the earth looking for a human who will exchange eternal godly authority for self-satisfying temporary power, as Esau did with desiring Jacob's stew more than the generational inheritance of his father. Even as mature intercessors, we often get caught up in a needless war with the adversary. He pits us against one another and laughs. But in prayer, we outrank him because of Christ. We do not fight with arrows of accusation but with forgiveness and prophetic declaration. To have the confidence to manifest the kingdom of God in moments or places of crisis, we must be eternally secure, have our gaze fixed like flint, and be resistant to man's opinions.

Heaven's Layers

An understanding of heaven's layers—the three levels of heaven we pray from—helps us access the proximity to God we need to intercede with power and authority. From the earthly realm, to the spiritual realm, to the ultimate destination of the throne of God, the three levels of heaven provide profound insights into the power of prayer and declaration, enabling us to abide with Jesus and reckon with the enemy in the unseen war.

Although we'll explore each level of heaven in detail, let's start with the highest, the throne of God, which is in the third heaven. Being taken up into the third heaven, a profound spiritual experience described in Scripture, is not only shocking but strategic when it comes to winning the spiritual war and manifesting the promises of God.

In 2 Corinthians 12:2–4, the apostle Paul speaks of a man being caught up to the third heaven. He shares that he was "caught up into paradise, and heard unspeakable words, which it is not lawful for a man to utter" (KJV). This indicates that being taken up into the third heaven involves encountering the glorious presence of God and receiving divine revelations that are beyond human comprehension and expression. Through this heavenly encounter, we are granted glimpses into the mysteries of God's kingdom and are invited to work in prayer from the eternal realm.

The book of Revelation also speaks of this realm when John is invited to come up to heaven (4:1–2), where he is transported in the Spirit and witnesses God's throne, heavenly worship, and the unfolding of end-time events. John's experience involved an unearthly journey into the spiritual realm and heavenly realities. From this, you and I can learn that we, too, are invited to enter through the "open door of heaven" to gain deeper insights into God's plans and purposes.

Though our experience may not be bodily like Paul's or John's, we do have access to spiritually abide with Christ in this realm. Strategic intercession stems from the clear revelation of scriptural truths. I can't stress this enough: Where we pray *from* matters, and agreement with Him matters. How can we agree if we cannot see from an eternal perspective?

Let's briefly dive into all the layers we traverse when we pray. Notice specifically where you get to pray *from* and how the authority you have been given increases your understanding of how the spirit realm is set up.

The first level of heaven represents the physical realm, the visible world we inhabit. It is the realm of earthly experiences and challenges, yet it's also where the redeemed have reign and dominion. In this level, we encounter trials, temptations, feelings, needs, lack, and the enemy's deceptions. We could say this is where we are aware of the gap between the promises of God and their fulfillment. However, through prayer, we commune with God and seek His guidance, strength, promises, and protection.

Unfortunately, in the earthly realm, many release their petitions from their spiritually blind, fallen nature. They have little desire for personal repentance or for the Lord to expose their unforgiveness. At worst, they want things better and to go their way; at best, the petition is for someone's problem to be fixed. The fallen nature is myopic and soulish. These prayers are not *bad* but immature; they can lack faith, power, and assurance in God's faithfulness. Sometimes prayers are sent from this place with a pure heart because pain is intense in our earthly realm. We are mainly focused on relief from our afflictions, highlighting anxiousness, worry, and lack. Again, these are not bad intercessions, but they are often either methodical or filled with frustration, blocking the fresh hope the Lord wants to give. The good news is that God loves to work in our weaknesses. He welcomes any petitions we bring before Him.

Truthfully, most of us begin our cry to God from a place of lack, need, or pain. He loves vulnerability—we just can't stay there if we want to tap into prayer that changes things. We must allow pain to press us into raw petitions of faith, grab the hem of His garment like the woman with the issue of blood, and praise Him for hearing our cries of vulnerability and believing He wants to heal our wounds. If we move from pain into confession, brokenness, and repentance, our eyes are opened to see heaven's strategies and holy hope. Here, we begin to find comfort, peace, and victory in the sovereignty of God. In this realm, the key is this: Repentance and praise move us from the first layer, earth, into the second layer, that of the spirit.

The second layer of heaven is the unseen spirit realm, where spiritual warfare unfolds. In this realm, our prayers become weapons of warfare, enabling us to perceive the accuser of the brethren as the father of lies and evil. Here, we engage in prayer and authoritative declarations, realize the power and authority given to us by Christ, declare the truth of God's Word, rebuke the demonic enemy, and proclaim God's promises over our lives.

Knowing your identity as a son of God exposes your heart to victory in the second layer of heaven. Most who grasp their spiritual warfare but not sonship get stuck here in an unnecessary demonic fight. They spend much of their time fighting the enemy and demon hunting instead of passing through this demonic place with their sonship badge. Those who know their identity rebuke the enemy when they discern the Lord putting those words in their mouths, but simultaneously, they keep their eyes locked on Jesus, press into the throne, and they sit down in their seat with Him. In this realm, the key is this: Don't get stuck in the warfare zone. It's not necessarily where the war is won. Calm your soul and keep moving toward the throne.

The third layer of heaven, as I discussed earlier, is the highest and most glorious dimension, the abode of God's presence, power, throne, and victory. Satan and the fallen angels were kicked out of this realm, which we can only enter by the blood of Jesus. Revelation 4:1 describes the apostle John being invited to come up to this heavenly realm. In this place, our prayers and declarations, fueled by the insight given through the Holy Spirit, come boldly to the throne of grace, ascend before the throne of God, and behold Him. All warfare seems to disappear here. His glory eclipses momentary afflictions. Our words rise as fragrant incense, pleasing to the Lord. In this holy realm, we experience intimacy with God, aligning our hearts with His purposes and receiving supernatural breakthroughs and answers to our prayers. In this realm, the key is to reign with Christ from this place. Pray for the kingdom to come and the will of God to be done in the earthly realm as it has been written in the scrolls of heaven. Lock eyes with Him because the accuser has been thrown down.

The three layers of heaven give us an understanding of the power of prayer and declaration. In the face of accusations, we rise above the enemy in the earthly realm through prayer, seeking God's wisdom, strategy, Word, and protection. In the spiritual realm, we engage in warfare, boldly declaring God's truth and refusing and rebuking the enemy's lies and accusations with the alive and active Word of God. And as we reach the highest layer of heaven, our prayers ascend before the throne, bringing forth speedy maturity, divine intervention, transformation, and the manifestation of the power and governmental authority of the kingdom. In most cases, in the third heaven, our feet are in the dirt of earth, but our spirits are engaged with the Lord. Here, we become skilled snipers in the prophetic and in prayer. Here, from our Ephesians 2:6 seat, He aims, we shoot, and He hits the intended target.

We gain strength and unwavering faith as messengers, leaders, mothers, fathers, sons, and daughters as we learn to operate as Jesus did.

Very truly I tell you, the Son can do nothing by himself; he can do only what he sees his Father doing, because whatever the Father does the Son also does. For the Father loves the Son and shows him all he does. Yes, and he will show him even greater works than these, so that you will be amazed. For just as the Father raises the dead and gives them life, even so the Son gives life to whom he is pleased to give it.

—John 5:19–21 NIV

In this, we unlock the miraculous as we live out brokenness, humility, victory, prayer, deliverance, and prophecy according to His flawless plan. When prayers don't yield the expected outcome, we trust His perfect leadership, timing, and knowledge of things to come. Abiding in Him unveils our role as immortal agents on a mission to usher His kingdom into this decaying world. The fullness of prayer's power lies in unraveling the depths of God's heart and His ordained plans in heaven's unseen scrolls.

Psalm 139:16 assures us, "Your eyes saw my unformed substance; in your book were written, every one of them, the days that were formed for me, when as yet there was none of them" (ESV). This verse underscores God's intimate knowledge and foresight in our lives. He is assuring us that all our days have been written in His book before we even came into existence, strengthening our faith.

Abiding in our heavenly seat with Him, we make eternity more tangible than the transient decay of the world.

An Encounter in the Courtroom

I've experienced firsthand the work that can be done by ascending heaven's layers. Once, I was in prayer and taking generational sins before the Lord to break them by the blood of Jesus. The deliverance prayer assignment was simple: Go before the throne of God and ask Him to open the books and ask the Holy Spirit to show any unrepented sin or areas the enemy had charged judgment against me or my family line. Suddenly, I knew I was in a similar scene to the following:

> I watched till thrones were put in place,
> And the Ancient of Days was seated;
> His garment was white as snow,
> And the hair of His head was like pure wool.
> His throne was a fiery flame,
> Its wheels a burning fire;
> A fiery stream issued
> And came forth from before Him.
> A thousand thousands ministered to Him;
> Ten thousand times ten thousand stood before Him.
> The court was seated,
> And the books were opened.
>
> —Daniel 7:9–10 NKJV

I was shocked at my response to this vision-like encounter with the Ancient of Days. I could feel the presence of angels all around me and the holiness of God inside and out. I was not afraid as one under judgment but awestruck as one who had finally laid eyes on the love of her life. He took the scrolls with all the accusations against me—I rejoiced! Satan was mocking me, exposing moments when I unknowingly aligned with his schemes regarding generational divorce, early death, and the lasting effects of sexual abuse. This left me feeling momentarily helpless, overwhelmed by despair, and utterly exhausted. However, as I began speaking forgiveness over myself and others, the sting of the enemy's accusations diminished.

The accuser presented his case against me and my family line; he wanted to use my testimony of how they wronged me against them. He aimed to reap these curses from my unforgiveness or careless words onto my children and their children. But I was so overtaken by the beauty of the Ancient of Days; He gazed at me with a smile as if He knew my response. When my eyes met His, I wept with amazement, ran past the accuser, and said, "It's you! It's you! You are so beautiful! Can I hug you?"

I didn't wait for a response, and He smiled as I ran boldly to His throne, pleading the blood of Jesus and thanking Him for His mercy. Neither He nor I cared about the accuser's case—my love for Him was so strong, and my desire to be in His arms was greater than my shame. Then I wept and declared to Him, "No, I repent and break agreement with this accuser and bless those who have cursed me. I bless them to know you and the beauty of your majesty. I plead the blood of the Lamb and declare that my testimony is Jesus and He made a way to come to you! I just want you. I just want them to know you!" He rebuked the accuser like He did for Joshua the high priest in Zechariah but spoke my name and that of my family's instead of Joshua's.

> Then the angel showed me Joshua the high priest standing before the angel of the LORD, with Satan standing at his right hand to accuse him. And the LORD said to Satan: "The LORD rebukes you, Satan! Indeed, the LORD, who has chosen Jerusalem, rebukes you! Is not this man a firebrand snatched from the fire?"
>
> —Zechariah 3:1–2 BSB

This profound encounter and the blessings spoken over those who once caused me pain transformed my life and theirs.

I witnessed the very prayers I had long agonized over come to fruition. The discord in my marriage gave way to romance and genuine intimacy, and my parents' health improved while they grew closer. No longer did I live in constant fear of my children falling prey to sexual abuse; I trusted in the Lord's protection.

This intercession is a type of deliverance, but it's not a one-time event; it is a way of life, a profound level of intimacy we can access, setting bloodlines free from demonic oppression and sin cycles. Intercession is a sacred place of sonship where we commune with the unseen and experience the splendor of hidden realms. We understand that there is more to this than just addressing family wounds or healing generational scars, though these are important. At maturity, intercession is about divine alignment, communion with God, and eternal joy. We are willing to accept the invitation to the humblest yet powerful position, seated alongside Christ in governing authority. We ascend to a realm that allows us to bring order to the chaos of the fallen world. We mature in our prayer life, stepping into meetings with the General of the Army in the heavenly war room. By acquiring intelligence and strategies, we can reclaim stolen territory.

In this journey, we find the same joy and confidence that our Father has in Psalm 2:1–6 when He laughs at the rage of the nations against Him. We become like the Proverbs 31 woman, laughing without fear of the future (Proverbs 31:25), for we've embraced our calling to govern with Christ.

LET'S ENCOUNTER

In the hidden battle, the enemy stands ready to hurl accusations, seeking to ensnare you in chaos. Let's declare together, "I will not surrender my holy authority to the enemy. My words shall breathe life and bring order to this chaotic world. I will dwell with Christ in the realm of peace."

Always remember, even in moments of pain or silence, your authority remains mighty, rooted in your position alongside Christ. As a child of God, your experiences in His presence grant you extraordinary revelation. When you pray from the throne of God, that third level of heaven, you become a vessel for Christ's redemption to flow into the world. It's time to activate your divine authority.

Pray with Me

Lord, I want to enjoy the unseen realm and not be afraid. Prayer can feel weak in the midst of this broken world and even in the battleground of the second heaven. Search my heart, reveal my need for repentance, and instill within me your humility and authority. Equip me with a profound understanding of your Word and the unwavering confidence to claim victory over the spiritual forces against us. Teach me to dwell in you continually.

May the words I speak and my thoughts be holy and powerful in your sight and within the spiritual realm. Help me grasp my eternal nature and the ability to ascend to the highest heavens in prayer. Unveil the depth and significance of my intercession, infusing my prayers with a spiritual language that dismantles the adversary and resounds powerfully in the ears of heaven. Amen.

7

ABIDING, BEHOLDING, AND DEVELOPING HOLY GRIT

Abide in Me, and I in you. As the branch cannot bear fruit of itself, unless it abides in the vine, neither can you, unless you abide in Me.

—John 15:4 NKJV

Hopefully, this book is helping you understand the wordless frustration and intercession you have begun to embody—the key, however, is ascending beyond the anguish and asking for God's heart in each circumstance. Abiding in Him sustains abandoned affection and a spirit of compassion in times of trial and tribulation. Jesus was moved with compassion when He healed and even when He flipped tables in the temple. As long as we are on assignment on this earth, our ministry is one of reconciliation, and His kingdom is one of righteousness, peace, and joy—especially when we shed holy tears.

Our King dwells in glory and splendor, and His joy is our strength. We must move beyond striving to enter glory, splendor, and moments of joy. No longer will He allow His people to grin and bear it. Holy grit is found in the place of rest. We outlast the enemy when we know we are beloved, not by our determination. We train our mind, will, and emotions through holy rest and abiding in the place of ascent where our redeemed spirit already dwells.

Let me say this plainly: Striving to abide is not abiding at all. A branch does not try to abide in a vine or groan and strain to bear fruit. Your spirit was created to live with Jesus above the warfare and rage of the nations.

The Chokehold of Worry

The Lord once spoke to my heart, "You visit heaven often in dreams and visions. When you sleep, I unveil many mysteries, strategies, and my heart because you are at rest in me. But you don't remember most of it because when you wake up, you allow the worries and cares of this world to choke out what I have shown you."

Mark 4:19 says it this way, "But the worries of this life, the deceitfulness of wealth, and the desires for other things enter and choke the word, and it becomes unfruitful."

The bride of Christ will not remain faithful through trials if she cannot rest in her heavenly seat. Even if she gains strategy, comfort, authority, power, and peace, she will quickly become distracted and dismantled by the panic of this world.

We have been invited and positioned to live in the splendor of the King. If we are going to have lasting endurance, walk in holy boldness, and speak the costly truth in the face of adversity, we must learn to "ascend the hill of the Lord" and command our soul to "be still and be seated."

120

Your prayer life can and will open closed gates so that the King of Glory can enter and bring forth His desires, but striving, fear, and worry must die if you are going to transition yourself and others into the holy endurance needed for the end of the age and manifest glory. Holy tears will not end on this side of eternity but are a segue into the greater works promised. Tears, travail, and trust cause mountains to move and the spotless bride to provoke the King to open heavenly gates that have long been sealed (see Psalm 24:7–10). As you learn to ascend, abide, and rest you will shift from groaning in the gap to holding the promise in your arms with joy.

Still, you must train your thought life, desires, and emotional responses to rise above the strife, warfare, and debilitating fear of the unredeemed realm. When the weeping comes upon us, it is a segue to feel brokenness, to align with the more excellent vision of heaven and birth the will of God, but it is not the highest place of prayer. Weeping endures for the night, but joy comes in the morning (Psalm 30:5), and what is sown in tears is reaped in joy.

In Isaiah 40:29, the Lord promises, "He gives power to the weak, and to those who have no might He increases strength" (NKJV). In verse 31, He promises to the righteous an unveiling of the future glory of Christ, yet He requires patience in the waiting. He calls us to fix our eyes on Him amid trials and temptations. Waiting does not mean we anxiously tap our fingers on a desk while time passes, but we actively ascend above the constraints of *chronos* time to access the eternal joy of the Lord: "I lift up my eyes to the mountains—where does my help come from? My help comes from the LORD, Maker of heaven and earth" (Psalm 121:1–2 NIV). You must only be still and command your soul to rise above the chaos to meet Him in the place of peace.

You Will Forget Your Tears

The strength promised to us supersedes present suffering as we shift our vision and lifestyle beyond moments of affliction, injustice, and sin into the holy, limitless, and eternal. Sometimes we forget that when we are born again, we are born into eternal life, not just hanging out here in the crazy until this life's temporal body expires. The Bible says, "The wages of sin is death, but the gift of God is eternal life" (Romans 6:23 NKJV). Our spirit is at peace in its eternal existence now and forever, but sometimes we have to tell our mind, will, and emotions to get with the holy program. We can only access unconstrained joy when we understand the concept of limitless abiding.

When Nehemiah read the law, the people were grieved over their sin, but he charged the people, "Do not grieve, for the joy of the LORD is your strength" (Nehemiah 8:10 NIV). This joy that our Father gives provides a passageway through grief into peace and joy. He enables us to rise above the curse and sting of sin and death. Remember, the writer of Romans 8:18 wants us to get excited about what is beyond our present suffering and press into His limitless glory.

I will be honest; it took me years to understand how joy and the birth pangs of longing for His justice could abide together. I am very black-and-white in my thinking. Often, we create a neat little compartment for joy and connect it with circumstances. We say silly things like "Today was a good day, bless the Lord!" or "Everything went wrong today. I must have ticked someone off up there." I had to realize that abiding prayer is ascending through tears and groans into full access of His glory.

One night, as I stood in the shower, the Lord said, "The groan is a passageway like labor is unto birthing. The promise will come, and you will forget your tears." It was like a glory bomb went off in my soul! The seasons of groaning will not go away but are a segue into the intercession of joyful expectancy. If we don't know where we are going or that something is coming after the tears, we will faint and give up. Once we realize we are headed through the darkness to meet Him in the light of His garden, birth something with Him, and work with Him, we have hope. Beloved, hear me: The garden—not the pain—is the destination. You are about to begin abiding in His unconstrained joy through every season. In the garden, the bride enjoys co-dominion with the Bridegroom.

In the same way, we are the joyful reason He endured the cross, so it will be for those who have groaned with Him to lay down their lives at the end of the age. He is their reward, and great joy is their mark.

Do Not Be Moved

In the Song of Solomon 5–6, the bride endures a dark night of the soul. Many fail to realize that she is on a journey through rejection, brokenness, and misunderstanding to reign with her husband in His garden. He knocks on her chamber door to draw her out. Often we can get so caught up in the trauma of the season of groaning that we fail to see the intimate invitation to understand heavenly mysteries. Song of Solomon 5:2–7 is a prophetic story the Lord has used to help me understand how myopic I can be. As we've endured with Him, we have been involved in the prophetic timeline of the global bride. He's drawing us into mature love.

The Bridegroom is calling. How will the bride respond?

I sleep, but my heart is awake.
  A sound! My beloved is knocking:

123

"Open to me, my sister, my darling,
    my dove, my flawless one.
My head is drenched with dew,
    my hair with the dampness of the night."

I have taken off my robe—
    must I put it back on?
I have washed my feet—
    must I soil them again?
My beloved put his hand to the latch;
    my heart pounded for him.
I rose up to open for my beloved.
    My hands dripped with myrrh,
my fingers with flowing myrrh
    on the handles of the bolt.
I opened for my beloved,
    but he had turned and gone.
My heart sank at his departure.
    I sought him, but did not find him.
    I called, but he did not answer.

I encountered the watchmen on their rounds of the city.
They beat me and bruised me;
    they took away my cloak, those guardians of the walls.

Song of Solomon 5:2–7 BSB

At first glance, one might think, *Wow, He came to her and then left her to be beaten by the watchmen! Why would he tease her this way? Why would He allow her to be exposed and abused by those who are supposed to protect her? If this represents Christ and the church, I'm not sure I can trust His leadership.* Many who have longed for intimacy with Jesus at all costs have experienced this painful reality. They waited in their inner room, and when He came, they knew the risk of leaving that comfort, so they delayed. Having given every excuse, they finally chased Him with all their heart, only to be stripped bare and ridiculed. In the beginning, our love for Him is all about us. But a time comes when we will have to risk it all to position ourselves to access a deeper friendship with Him.

You may know your love and zeal for Him are pure and authentic. Don't be moved by the persecutions that you face; He is drawing you out for a greater purpose. Even when we delay, He works out all things for our good. God is about to unlock a mystery of this bridal drama: The Bridegroom says to her,

> *I have come to my garden*, my sister, my bride;
>   I have gathered my myrrh with my spice.
> I have eaten my honeycomb with my honey;
>   I have drunk my wine with my milk. . . .
> [Then the Bride says to the harlots in the street,] *My beloved has gone down to his garden*,
>   to the beds of spices,
> to pasture his flock in the gardens
>   and to gather lilies.
> *I belong to my beloved and he belongs to me*;
>   he pastures his flock among the lilies.

—Song of Solomon 5:1; 6:2–3 BSB, emphasis added

You Are Not Alone

God never abandons His beloved. Remember, you are not alone. He always pulls us into a more lavish entrance to Himself. He longs to offer us more grace for the assignment. Before the pain and abuse of the watchmen, He tells her to open to Him, and when she delays, she knows where He has been and where He is going. His knock at her door is an invitation for her to fully identify as His wife and co-laborer. In this hour, the bride of Christ is being drawn out of her chamber, grappling with immaturity but being led into His garden, where He offers us more than a mechanical organization called church. In her statement to the women in the street, she reveals she knew where He was all along. She just wanted to play it safe in the comfort of her house.

Her lovesick desire to find Him motivates the harlots to ask to know Him. As she is exposed, she remains unoffended. Yet her unveiling revealed her true identity as His. "For the eagerly awaiting creation waits for the revealing of the sons and daughters of God" (Romans 8:19).

I Am My Beloved's

After Jayden was healed, some of those I expected to celebrate did not. Some did not accept the miracle, and others were intimidated by the new level of healing anointing that rested on our family. I became intensely broken and somewhat confused. I knew Jesus drew our family out of our chamber and away from ministry *about* us to the power of the Gospel resting *on* us for His glory.

But this miracle seemed to take us into a deep dark night of the soul. During a powerful time of worship, I sat with my back against the wall and groaned deep guttural cries before the Lord. Suddenly I cried, "I don't understand! I refuse to be offended! I want you!"

The Lord told me, "If they knew who you were, they wouldn't have beaten you. But you know who you are. Come into my garden!"

The revelation hit my soul with a bolt of lightning, and I cried in response, "If they had known who she was, they wouldn't have beaten her. But she knew who she was: the king's wife."

Because she knew who she was and where she was going, no offense was found in her.

Unending Oil and Fire

Our oil must increase; no, it must be unending. Abiding in intimacy with the Lord and living without offense and above accusation lead to endless oil, ever-kindled fire, and seeing the glory of the Lord in the land of the living.

In Matthew 25:1–13, Jesus shares a parable about ten virgins and their end-time wake-up call. To those in attendance, He emphasizes the waiting; to us, He emphasizes the urgency of the hour we live in.

> At that time the kingdom of heaven will be like ten virgins who took their lamps and went out to meet the bridegroom. Five of them were foolish and five were wise. The foolish ones took their lamps but did not take any oil with them. The wise ones, however, took oil in jars along with their lamps. The bridegroom was a long time in coming, and they all became drowsy and fell asleep.
>
> —Matthew 25:1–5 NIV

First of all, you must have oil in your lamp. We've already discussed how the brokenness and pressing you have walked through produce oil and anointing as you refuse to become hard, bitter, or offended and you open your soul to the Lord. Let Him peel back the layers as He pleases. But mature oil is costly. Acquiring it involves digging deep into the Word, abiding in prayer, refusing offense, and longing for the mysteries of God. The wise reach beyond identity as His children or even as fivefold ministers.

> You ought to be teachers . . . For everyone who partakes only of milk is unacquainted with the word of righteousness, for he is an infant. But solid food is for the mature, who because of practice have their senses trained to distinguish between good and evil.
>
> —Hebrews 5:12–14

When we hunger for Him in every season, we store oil and continue burning even when we are sleeping. In Matthew 25, we see that all ten virgins fell asleep. The Lord establishes seasons of waiting and encourages rest. The prudent continue to burn through the night season because they are never satisfied with one encounter and do not allow difficulty to jade them. But the foolish could be compared to the Christian who said the sinner's prayer once, prays in tongues once or twice a month, goes to church most Sundays, and may be on a ministry staff. Unfortunately, they think they have seen it all, done it all, and can coast through the rest of life on the old oil from the "glory days."

The foolish one looks at the burning messenger and is annoyed by what they consider excess. But when the trumpet sounds, all will wake up from their slumber, and the foolish will realize their lamp is dim and their oil is gone. Let this not be you. Never believe you have arrived. Always ask for more. Always be willing to reassess your relationship with the Lord. Let pruning take place and learn to move with the wind of the Spirit in all seasons.

Dear burning one, your oil is not for sale now nor will it be when the trumpet sounds. It is time to dive deeper into intimacy with God. Maybe your holy grit will provoke the foolish to buy oil before it's too late.

Waiting on the Wedding

The groan of the Spirit within is for us to know we are His sons and daughters, for our revealing, and for the glorious wedding when we forever reign with our Bridegroom (Romans 8:15).

God is inviting us to abide in rest with Him yet labor into a new place of prayer and bold preaching. First, we must become aware of our dullness. Ask Him for greater compassion and even intercessory tears for the scoffers. Our hearts are broken, but we must press our ears to the heart of Jesus. We must never water down the wine of His glory, nor repent of extravagant worship, heaven-rending prayer, or bold proclamation of His Word.

He is bidding us to ask again to be taught how to pray. We must sit with Him in heavenly realms and dialogue about how to work with Him in prayer.

The fiercest intercessors among us have only tapped into the equivalent of one grain of sand of the revelation of God. Jesus's lifestyle of prayer was the most provoking reality to His friends. I want it to provoke me as well. I want to learn to pray from my seat in the heavenlies and never again from a place of defeat.

I prophesy that the Lord is moving His people from *building* the house of prayer to *being* the house of prayer, from praying the Scriptures to manifesting them because they have learned to abide face-to-face with Him.

In Matthew 22, Jesus describes what it will be like when His return is near. There is a wedding; His messengers go to the religious community to invite them to the banquet. These prophets are beaten and murdered as they proclaim the master's coming. Those invited are annoyed, preoccupied, and stubborn. Because they are violent, are unwilling to shift their focus, and refuse the call to come to celebrate the marriage, the master burns their city and sends new messengers. He says to the prophets, "'The wedding banquet is ready, but those I invited were not worthy. Go therefore to the crossroads and invite to the banquet as many as you can find.' So the servants went out into the streets and gathered everyone they could find, both evil and good, and the wedding hall was filled with guests" (v. 8–10 BSB).

The outcasts, rebels, and unbelievers receive the invitation to come in place of the religious. Matthew 22 was fulfilled when Israel was cut off and the Gentiles were grafted into the kingdom through Christ. But it was also a prophetic Scripture predicting a time before the return of the Lord when much of Christendom would reject the warnings of modern servants of the Lord.

In our current climate, the mandate is being given to compel the rebels and outcasts to come into the kingdom. True prophets have called the church to return to intimacy with God in the last decade. These wilderness voices have prophesied with tears of judgment, global shaking, and the Lord's desire for mercy and to gather people to Himself.

Many have gone spiritually underground in America because they are sick of spiritual compromise, political mixture, and the status quo. These voices hunger and thirst for righteousness and the pure presence of God. After much pressure from the enemy to conform to woke culture or religious box-checking, they quit the system. Yet they are leading an internal revolution against the antichrist system. But be warned, some counterfeits talk the talk of a new wineskin but are in rebellion against the Word and holiness of God. Purity is not legalism but a requirement to enter God's kingdom. May our discernment be sharper now than ever. So many need healing, especially from church hurt, but woundedness left unaddressed becomes bitterness and rebellion against God.

The true underground Church did not quit on the truth; they died to their agendas. Instead, they have been ravenously consuming the Scriptures, seeking truth, living in brokenness, and abiding in the face of God. They are hosting His presence in their hearts and homes and preparing their spouses and children for the best of times and the worst of times. The rebels are hosting unholy alliances and drinking parties, leading the flock into sin, and calling themselves Christian communities.

The true reformers resemble the Lamb on the throne; their eyes radiate His presence and compassion, and they walk in consecration. When we die with Him as broken vessels, we embody the message we preach. (See Revelation 5.) Their lifestyle will compel the lost to ask, "Who is your beloved? Tell us that we may love Him too."

Radical faith comes from hearing the Word of God. Jesus is the Word, and He has given us full access to His heart, throne, and mysteries. I tell you, many who thought they were abiding will soon realize they became lazy virgins. They believe they have arrived, but their lamps will quickly burn out. May we be so relentless in our pursuit of knowing Him that we refuse to believe the lie that we have arrived at the complete understanding of prayer, the Church, and the Scriptures.

In this hour, by becoming a house of prayer instead of only building a house of prayer, the bride will transform into a white-hot consecrated message of the Bridegroom's coming. The groan of the Spirit within is the genesis of faithful witnesses across the earth, a groan for His people who would rise up and speak fearlessly about His revelations in prayer and in the Word and who would build His prevailing Church.

The River of Life Flowing from His Temple

As we move closer to the most significant revival the world has ever seen, His return, He is whispering the hidden mysteries of His kingdom to those close to His heart. Out of our innermost beings will flow the rivers of living water as we gaze on Him.

In Ezekiel 47:8, the river of God flows from the temple, and in John 7:38, the river flows from the people of God. The Holy Spirit readily abides in us, longing to produce the living fruit to manifest the kingdom in stagnant wilderness places. In other words, you and I are positioned as priests before Him, living stones, and we are His temple, not metaphorically but literally (see 1 Peter 2:5–9). The river that flows from the abiding witness of Christ is life and life abundant. In the same way that physical Babylon was destroyed once and will be spiritually once and for all, literal and spiritual rivers will flow, bringing life where there once was death. "Behold, I am going to do something new, now it will spring up; will you not be aware of it? I will even make a roadway in the wilderness, rivers in the desert" (Isaiah 43:19).

As with all prophetic Scripture, God speaks literally of lands, cities, stones, and so forth but desires for us to grasp the profoundly personal mysteries of how the cross of Christ made us His temple, His living stones, and His city. The fullness of prophecy revealed is in Christ and His bride reaching beyond this broken earthly existence.

> The one who overcomes I will make a pillar in the temple of My God, and he will never again leave it. Upon him I will write the name of My God, and the name of the city of My God (the new Jerusalem that comes down out of heaven from My God), and My new name.
>
> —Revelation 3:12 BSB

We are like rocks that have not yet realized we are pillars in the house of God. The urgency of the hour demands that you and I understand who we are and what we build when we pray and open our mouths. He has mysteries to unveil to equip us as His faithful witnesses. When I began this book, I wrote of the unspoken prayers gripping people to lay down their lives. Romans 8:18–19 speaks of the unveiling of the sons of God. These are mysteries. In Scripture, the word *mystery* is something we can grasp and understand. He longs to share with us, empower us, and send us out.

John marvels at the mystery of the beast because he is a student of the Old Testament and knows only hints concerning the harlot and the beast. He was experiencing the revealing of a mystery at that moment. You've probably heard it said that "the New Testament is the Old Testament revealed." When we travail with the Spirit, we are aligned with heaven's answers. We transform into the message we preach; we become a lightning rod demonstrating the living Christ.

Signs and Wonders Are Not Optional

Healing is not simply a *good idea*; ask anyone crying out for a child to live. Speaking in tongues is not a Pentecostal badge; ask someone who heard, and accepted, the Gospel for the first time in their own language from a missionary who was speaking in tongues. Raising the dead is not something spooky or an excellent idea; ask the wife whose husband died and God brought him back to her when she groaned and prayed. Signs and wonders are not optional or radical; they are biblical. Cessation is heresy, and trying to turn these into formulas is arrogant. Let the Scriptures speak for themselves.

These signs will accompany those who have believed: in My name they will cast out demons, they will speak with new tongues; they will pick up serpents, and if they drink any deadly poison, it will not harm them; they will lay hands on the sick, and they will recover.

—Mark 16:17–18 ESV

People will abuse the Word of God. Satan will counterfeit the supernatural. But you and I do not need to worry about that. Remember, worry will cause us to forget His secrets that He unveils. We must believe and abide in Him, and the fruit will burst forth. You and I get the pleasure of bearing with Him in His grief, feeling His compassion, and allowing Him to move through us to demonstrate His fame.

As the time of the Lord's return draws near, so will His power and anointing increase, as will the simultaneous pressure to hide the gifts. In many nations, releasing the miraculous in the name of Jesus will cost you your life. So praise the Lord and manifest His kingdom now. As Galatians 6:10 says, "Therefore, as we have opportunity, let us do good to everyone, and especially to the family of faith" (BSB).

LET'S ENCOUNTER

You are seated above the whirlwind of the enemy and the strife of the times, but you must learn how to abide. Let's move into the fullness of joy that is not constrained by circumstance yet accessed by rising above fear-driven anxiety. Christ promises His strength to you as you learn to wait on Him and abide. Remember, your spirit is already seated with Him in the place of peace. Your new level of intercession is producing the grit to buy costly oil that burns within even on the darkest night. As a burning messenger, you are gaining strategy and mysteries of heaven that have eternal implications. Be still and listen for His heart—its go time.

PRAY WITH ME

Dear God, thank you for providing the spiritual strength required to endure my fears as I strive faithfully. I can be at ease and know that although I may faint and grow weary, you never will. Let the teaching of my rightful place in your kingdom go deep and grow into an oak tree of righteousness in my soul. Help me know that as I sit and rest in you, the war is already won. Amen.

8

THERE'S A SWORD
IN YOUR MOUTH

God and the devil, opposing forces of good and evil, life and death, truth and deception, seek to govern the earth, beginning with you.

—Dutch Sheets, *Authority in Prayer*

Our words have the power to ignite hearts, transform lives, shape destinies, end wars, and set captives free. I often cry out that we could learn to speak with the fervor of heaven, for in our words we carry the essence of God's truth and love, awakening a sleeping world to the power of redemption and revival. Hebrews 4:12 says, "For the word of God is living and active, sharper than any two-edged sword, piercing to the division of soul and of spirit, of joints and of marrow, and discerning the thoughts and intentions of the heart" (ESV). If His Word is in our mouths, we can indeed transform the earth.

I knew the true story the movie *The Sound of Freedom* was based on before I watched it. But I wondered if I was ready to see the story on screen based on the response of my body, soul, and spirit. I was inundated with intense emotions and feelings I struggled to verbalize. In many ways, it's my story too. Afterward, I became heavy-laden: Was this post-traumatic stress disorder (PTSD)? Was I angry with the lack of intercession and involvement from the body of Christ to set the captives free? I could not put my finger on what was going on in my soul.

To make the burden worse, the next morning, I opened my phone to see two child traffickers' Instagram accounts had *liked* my photos. I blocked and reported them. I wanted to vomit and knew the demonic was at work. But why? Satan does not attack without a purpose. Amid the whirlwind of emotions, I began listening for the whispers of God.

The tragedies and atrocities in this world are often so horrific, yet we strive to ignore them because they exceed the capacity of our emotions. We may try to shut down the feelings and run from the pain. But if we know our calling is upward, we can lean into the groan and ask for the purpose.

Later, during the church service, when we began to sing out the name of Yeshua, all I could do was groan and pant out the world's despair, anger, and fury over child trafficking. I was nearly breathless.

I thought, *What will I do? How will I speak of this burden? How will I reply when I am questioned about my story?* Soon, the anger and the accuser's questioning hit: Why was I undefended? How did I escape when millions of children and teens were enslaved? Then, I remembered my mother's prayer: *"Rip her out!"* She'd had no idea what I needed to be ripped out of, only that Satan was at work. Her prayers were sent like warfare burrowing underground, unseen by the enemy, to set me free.

This is the key: We must use a deep inner groan to damage the enemy and allow God to change history. We reject the accusations, use the triggers to find healing, and quickly turn the enemy's attacks on him. That Sunday morning, I was under attack but so were little children worldwide. Would I transform my wordless anguish and questions into intercession? As I cried in tongues, it was as if I felt the trauma of every trafficked child and the Lord's indignation over the abuse of His children. I had a sword in my mouth and was determined to fight to wake up the sleeping bride and for captive children to be set free. I turned my pain into intercession. Through my weeping, the Lord prayed through me: "Rip them out of the clutches of Satan. Return the babies to their families, free the captives, and awaken your bride."

Then the Lord unveiled prophetic revelation to my soul: "My church is the sole barrier between these children and the antichrist. She must come out of the influence of the spirit of Babylon and take her post! Cry for my bride!"

I cried, declared, and sang: "Wake up, sleeping church! Stop looking at yourself and your platforms. Wake up and roar! Time to set free the captives!" Intercession continued, encompassing all spiritual languages. When I got up from that altar, I fully expected to see news headlines of trafficking busts and intercessory teams stepping up to cover those fighting on the frontlines of this rescue mission—and I did. The very next day, my husband read an article to me about a trafficking bust in our own state!

How Will You Wield Your Sword?

We must be aware of the impact of our words in relation to our prayers. Consider Jesus's disciples, who were stunned by the power and significance of His prayer life, His wisdom, and His ability to bridle His tongue. As they witnessed the results of His prayers, they prodded Jesus not to teach them to preach a powerful message, to shut down the religious spirit, or to move in the miraculous, but to teach them to pray. His response is this:

In this manner, therefore, pray:

> Our Father in heaven,
> Hallowed be Your name.
> Your kingdom come.
> Your will be done
> On earth as it is in heaven.
> Give us this day our daily bread.
> And forgive us our debts,
> As we forgive our debtors.
> And do not lead us into temptation,
> But deliver us from the evil one.
> For Yours is the kingdom and the power and the glory
> forever. Amen.

—Matthew 6:9–13 NKJV

God commands us to pray and prophesy, wielding the sword in our mouths that His will be done.

Be aware that Satan also wants to use the words of our mouths and will hijack our mind, body, spirit, and soul to influence and enact the tongue as a powerful instrument for evil. The accuser of the brethren (Revelation 12:10) uses our fleshly desires, shortcomings, and brothers and sisters to convince us that God is not trustworthy. His aim is to extinguish the holy fire and hunger within us; his mission is to visit the courts of heaven day and night, causing chaos for those in Christ.

As we explored earlier, we must understand that we are in a war, and warriors must know their enemy's strategies and hiding places. We must anticipate the actions of our enemy. He is like a roaring lion seeking whomever he may devour (1 Peter 5:8). In the day that evil comes, we will stand our ground (Ephesians 6:13).

One key to overcoming the enemy and reserving our mouths for God's purposes is praying for wisdom, discernment, godly longing, and consecration. James affirms the tongue as one of the most potent spiritual power instruments—tiny, but mightily capable of blessing or cursing (James 3:10). He calls it the unruliest member. We can't tame it ourselves but must do so with a bit and bridle through walking in the fear of the Lord. Therefore, we must pray and beckon the wisdom of heaven, which is "pure; then peace-loving, considerate, submissive, full of mercy and good fruit, impartial and sincere" (James 3:17 NIV).

Through this wisdom and by aiming to live peacefully, we can resist firing back when others accuse us; we can be quick to forgive. With every offense, we can run to the mercy seat of God. We know accusations and insults will still come. But when it rains and pours, God has equipped us with grace and gifts to fortify us in our weakness. We can learn to give the Lord our shortcomings, repent of our wrongdoing, plead the blood of Jesus, and receive mercy and grace instead of falling prey to the enemy.

> So Christ himself gave the apostles, the prophets, the evangelists, the pastors and teachers, to equip his people for works of service, so that the body of Christ may be built up until we all reach unity in the faith and the knowledge of the Son of

God and become mature, attaining to the whole measure of the fullness of Christ.

—Ephesians 4:11–13 NIV

As we consider the power of our mouths, we see that all the fivefold spiritual gifts presented in Ephesians—apostles, prophets, evangelists, pastors, and teachers—are speaking gifts. Also note the role of these gifts in building up Christ's body. We're meant to grow in spiritual maturity, as doing so allows us to steward these gifts in a way that draws us into fuller agreement with God.

We then see beyond momentary afflictions, learn to pace and discipline ourselves, and become like little children in our trust in the Lord. The accuser's voice begins to fade, and the voice of our Father becomes crystal clear. In this, we begin to take on His longing to evict the influence of evil from the earth. Injustice becomes less about us and more about taking hold of all that Jesus gave His life to apprehend. When we begin to meditate on and pray out the Scriptures and when we dialogue with Him, revelation and glory will come as well as holy frustration. We then start to grasp the groan of all creation (Romans 8:22).

We don't want to be landing strips for the enemy on earth; we want to be lightning rods for revival and conduits for the manifest presence of God. Out of the abundance of the heart, the mouth speaks (Matthew 12:34). If we long for God's presence, in many ways, we're experiencing an inner craving for sanctification and the restoration of our mouths to the place of dominion and authority.

The power of life and death resides in the tongue. The entire world was brought into existence by the spoken Word of God. We just explored how the ministry gifts outlined in

Scripture involve expressing words. We know the power of the mouth and that language carries spiritual significance. Yet there are various types of language in the Spirit, and each functions differently. Let's explore this arsenal of spiritual-language weapons we hold.

The Sniper Can Become the Stealth Bomber

The Holy Spirit gives tongues for prayer, worship, prophecy, and edification. This gift is like a sharpshooting sniper rifle. On Pentecost, believers spoke in tongues (Acts 2 and 1 Corinthians 12–14). Isn't it interesting that various tongues were the first gift on Pentecost and that Peter clarified what was happening to the crowd with Joel's prophecy afterward?

When we use the gift of tongues in prayer daily, we build up our spirit, we relocate our prayer position, and God responds to our petitions. As stated in 1 Corinthians 14:2, "For one who speaks in a tongue speaks not to men but to God; for no one understands him, but he utters mysteries in the Spirit" (ESV). Praying in tongues allows us to connect directly with God to align our hearts with His, express our deepest desires and needs, and hear His response, which is the unveiling of His mysteries to us. It is a powerful way to commune with Him, and He responds to the sincere cries of our hearts.

Jude admonishes us in Jude 1:19–20 to preserve by abiding in the spirit and praying in the spirit to break divisions. "These are the ones who cause divisions, who are worldly and devoid of the Spirit. But you, beloved, by building yourselves up in your most holy faith and praying in the Holy Spirit" (BSB). Praying in the spirit at all times, individually and collectively, aids in breaking divisions and bringing unity and harmony among believers.

But intercession alone will not align your heart; it is the access point to the heart of God, the opportunity to become humbled, and the substance of faith, but our actions must follow. We must learn to live in the Spirit in prayer and deed so that we do not give provision to the desires of our flesh, like selfishness and pride, which can hinder our prayers and relationships with others (see Galatians 5:16).

Two Types of Tongues and Their Functions: Intercession and Prophecy

Intercession (personal prayer in the Spirit) and tongues of prophecy are two types of tongues that have their own specialized functions in Scripture. In public places, such as churches or mission fields, intercession is often very personal and can be more like a sniper rifle than a machine gun. For the most potent personal strengthening, it operates best in hiddenness.

Still, snipers can gather in large prayer and worship groups to transform their sharpshooting rifles into heavenly stealth bombers. Spirit-led prayers and worship can unleash decisive victories in spiritual warfare when working as a group. First Corinthians 14 sheds light on the different types of tongues. While speaking in tongues without interpretation might lead to confusion, that does not negate the importance of Spirit-led intercession during a service.

Prophetic Tongues and the Power of the Holy Spirit

Both prophetic tongues with interpretation and personal tongues serve distinct purposes. Personal prayer in the Spirit, during worship, aligns our hearts with God's and sharpens our discernment as to the direction of His Spirit. However, we must, at times, harness the outward expression of these prayers to edify the church. This requires submission to the fear of the Lord, sensitivity to the direction of the Holy Spirit, humility, and an awareness of our motivations and desires.

Tongues of prophecy are meant to be understood, and they function like straightforward prophecies in the heavenly language and end with a native interpretation. Interpretation can come through a prayer, a spontaneous worship song, spontaneous revelation-driven preaching, or someone in the crowd hearing the word of the Lord and speaking it out in English or the native language of the crowd. Unfortunately, we often limit prophetic interpretation to a random person speaking out after the tongue.

Tongues of Intercession

On the other hand, there are tongues of intercession without interpretation, during which the focus should not be on being understood by others but instead on leading the interpretation flowing into Spirit-led prayers or songs or none at all. Often, when this begins, our minds are engaged chiefly with the wonder of God in worship and not focused on understanding the language of God.

Praying in tongues without pressing for interpretation allows the community of shared faith to come into alignment and communicate directly with God, invoking the ministry of the Holy Spirit to move heavenward. The whole room is focused on tuning into God and allowing Him to move through them in the service. Discipleship and relationship with one another are essential in these atmospheres to prevent misuse and confusion. Prophetic tongues with interpretation stir people's hearts, urging them to respond to heavenly directives.

Intense corporate prayer in the Spirit is best reserved for gatherings of like-minded believers, not necessarily evangelistic meetings attended by mostly unbelieving people, who can be confused. But stifling tongues altogether as a rule in services does not allow the spirit of prophecy or the power of God to drop and transform lives as it did in Acts. We lean on the Scriptures as our plumb line, including those we don't fully understand. We aren't in control; in Acts 2, no one was in control besides the Holy Spirit. Peter simply received an unction from the Lord to prophesy, according to Joel 2, explaining what was happening as thousands of people were speaking in different languages all at once.

As a thirteen-year-old Methodist girl, I went to a camp meeting where the gifts of the Spirit were in full function, not limited to but including tongues. I was not afraid. I was amazed at the tangible presence of God. I had no clue what was happening, but my heart beat wildly. I longed to run to the altar to meet Jesus, and I did. When I reached what felt like the threshold, a man walked up and began to pray for me in the Spirit. I fell to the floor, and people surrounded me in prayer. They prophesied over me. When I got up, I was never the same again. I knew in my gut that the Bible and all that it contained were real. The Holy Spirit marked me, and the power of God stayed with me. He began to teach me about Himself, even when I went back to my Methodist church and Baptist youth group. After I was filled with the Holy Spirit with the guidance of those unashamed Pentecostals, I fell in love with Jesus and His Word. My faith exploded.

This story illustrates how the use of tongues of prophecy can manifest in a gathering where unbelievers are present, leading to the conversion, healing, or deliverance of all who are in attendance. As we embrace different forms of tongues, our worship becomes a symphony of divine interaction—some for God's ears and some for man's. By understanding the distinction, we can fully appreciate and partake in the dynamic spiritual gifts available to us. As we fervently pursue both praying in tongues and promoting prophecy, the Holy Spirit will move mightily within and among us. We simply must ask for maturity and discernment to know when He wants us to be audible or silent.

If you have not received your prayer language, ask God for it, as you want Him to give you everything He has. When He comes, it will start with a wordless unction deep in your soul. Tell Him, "If this is you, give me all of yourself." For more about my personal experience and being baptized in the Holy Spirit, read *Permission to Burn*. Despite your initial babble, keep praying in faith. Prayer in the Spirit will transform your life, build your faith, and deepen your knowledge of the vastness of God.

If you already have your prayer language, use it "at all times" to stay tuned to the Holy Spirit's guidance and strengthen your relationship with God. This intimate connection will provide wisdom, discernment, and the ability to navigate divisions and worldly influences. Challenge yourself to pray in tongues every day.

The Lightsaber and Double-Edged Sword: Prophecy and Declaration

Prophecy is a spiritual language that God uses to communicate His messages and purposes to His people, and it is also used strategically in prayer as a declaration. Like a lightsaber, it divides the soul from the spirit and illuminates truth (see Hebrews 4:12). So true prophecy entails speaking God's Word, revelation, encouragement, correction, and intercession through the inspiration of the Holy Spirit. First Corinthians 14 describes the practice of prophecy for the purpose of strengthening and edifying the church.

A declaration in prayer is a powerful act of affirming and proclaiming God's promises and truth. By declaring God's Word, we activate our faith and invite God's intervention into our lives and circumstances. Scripture references for declaration in prayer include Mark 11:24, Psalm 107:28–30, and Romans 4:17.

Declaration in prayer has changed history by aligning the earth with God's purpose and will through faith-filled intercession, bringing forth transformation and miracles. You can take the Scriptures, combine them with faith in prayer, and declare truth over a situation. When doing this, you use your sword and apply the light to destroy the darkness.

In times of crisis or great need, historic declarations in prayer have led to significant shifts in events and nations. For example, King Hezekiah's prayer in 2 Kings 19:15–19 declared God's sovereignty and sought deliverance from the Assyrian threat, saving Jerusalem from destruction.

Rees Howells, known as the Intercessor, played a pivotal role during World War II through his fervent prayers and unwavering declarations. The book *Rees Howells: Intercessor* provides a firsthand story of how he and those at the Bible College of Wales (BCW) interceded on behalf of the British troops for their protection and victory. The war was won first and foremost on the battlefield of prayer, led by prayer warriors who fought the enemy on their knees.

In intercessory declaration, Howells and his students successfully steered through the Dunkirk crisis. His biographer, Norman Grubb, writes that throughout the war, "The whole college was in prayer every evening from 7 PM to midnight, with only a brief interval for supper. They never missed a day. This was in addition to an hour's prayer meeting every morning, and very often at midday. There were many special periods when every day was given up wholly to prayer and fasting."[1]

Grubb writes that Howells told his students: "Don't allow those young men at the front to do more than you do here." Over the Dunkirk period, he spent four days alone with God "to battle through and, as others have testified, the crushing burden of those days broke his body. He literally laid down his life."[2]

During the battle at Dunkirk, Howells got divine prayer assignments and treated them like military strategies from heaven. As the Lord revealed the directives, the intercessors fervently prayed for the British troops stranded on the beaches. He and those at the BCW declared with unwavering faith that they would be rescued and saved from the impending threat of the German forces. As the evacuation unfolded, against all odds, a remarkable turn of events occurred, and the rescue of more than three hundred thousand soldiers from Dunkirk took place, confirming to Rees and those at the BCW the power of their intercessions and the faithfulness of God to fulfill His promises through prayer.[3]

His testimony of Dunkirk stands as one of countless testaments to the miraculous impact of intercession during the war. For you and me, this story should pour oil on our fire to take our intercession to a new level—believing God for divine intelligence and laser-accurate declarations, powerful enough to turn the tide of the unseen war on our generation.

In Acts 4:29–31, early believers declared God's power and asked for boldness to share the Gospel despite persecution. Their prayer was answered, and the Holy Spirit filled them, leading to exponential growth in the early Church and changing the course of history. Through fervent declarations in prayer, we tap into the supernatural realm, ushering in the divine influence that can transform individual lives and shape the course of history itself. When the burden of the Lord is at its peak, often your wordless prayers can be transformed into divine intervention through powerful Spirit-led prophetic declarations. You only need to listen for His answer in the form of a verse, dream, or holy idea.

Jesus is the spirit of prophecy. Prophecy is a weapon derived from intimacy and a lifestyle of prayer through the Holy Spirit. Prophecy is also the gift of speaking God's oracles, which separate soul and spirit. You can know the Scriptures and engage with God consistently through intimacy and intercession, but be still and listen, as this is the first place where prophecy is formed. Prophecy is false, and can even be sorcery, without intimacy with God and knowledge of the Scriptures.

Vulnerability with God is the first step toward intimacy. Allow Him to know you fully. Knowing as you are known is a transcendent and soul-stirring concept that touches you at your very core. It speaks to your deep desire to fathom God and His ways and be fully understood and accepted, not just by others but by your Creator Himself. We long for a connection beyond mere surface knowledge—a connection that delves into the hidden recesses of our souls where our joys, sorrows, fears, and dreams reside.

Prophecy and revelation become powerful weapons as we immerse ourselves in the knowledge of God, engage in the fear of the Lord, and cry out to know His thoughts and desires and make them our own. As you aim to align your heart with His divine purpose and desire to see His will manifest, you will develop a keen ear for the voice of the Lord. But always remember your prophetic sword is personal before it is for others.

Prophetic Precision and Living as a Sacrifice

We receive authority in His kingdom when we prophesy and make divine declarations from brokenness and humility. We walk in the truth of Jesus's promise, "Blessed are the humble, for they will inherit the earth" (Matthew 5:5 CSB). When we allow the prophetic to fully expose our hearts, we will not be cast away for using His power because we lived to draw near to His heart.

> "Not everyone who says to me, 'Lord, Lord,' will enter the kingdom of heaven, but only the one who does the will of my Father who is in heaven. Many will say to me on that day, 'Lord, Lord, did we not prophesy in your name and in your name drive out demons and in your name perform many miracles?' Then I will tell them plainly, 'I never knew you; away from me, you evildoers!'"
>
> —Matthew 7:21–23 NIV

Knowing as we are known comes to full fruition in heaven, but for now, it is an invitation to be totally exposed to Him and set apart unto Him. When I think of inviting God to know me, I see a picture of a sacrifice on the altar. The sacrifice is dead and filleted open to be completely consumed by God. As we become living sacrifices, we open the deepest places of our souls and invite Him to consume them with His fire. We discover His desire for intimacy and His longing for our accuracy in prayer and prophecy.

Knowing is a two-way street: a call to expose our hearts and surrender to a love beyond human comprehension. We have access to His heart, and He, ours. We avoid becoming wounded prophets who only speak from a critical spirit or, even worse, veiled psychic readers on the road to the eternal lake of fire.

In the end, knowing Him forms the weapons of declaration and prophecy. These types of spiritual language are invitations to a profound spiritual victory with the power to shape history and our existence. Knowing and being known are keys to being accurate prophetically in prayer and preaching. In this way, we can use His words to move heaven and earth and become faithful messengers and lovesick worshipers with powerful prophetic precision.

Subterranean Warfare: Tears, Travail, and Intercession

Subterranean warfare is designed to burrow and hit the earth at high speed, penetrating the ground before exploding. The military can deliver such weapons by short-range missiles or aircraft intended to attack underground targets. Intercession is taught throughout this book; it comes in many forms.

The tears and travail of prayer serve as spiritual languages offered on behalf of others as supplications. In intercession, we often enter into compassionate spiritual identification with the pain and injustice of the wages of sin. Your tears and travails open the eyes of cities, nations, and people groups to the power of God. As with underground warfare, intercession gets close to the target and transforms the earth. Tears have language. Jesus wept a groan that brought resurrection life to Lazarus. Tears contain the power of compassion. Travail births what may have died in the birth canal. Through travail, we enter the labor pains of creation and agree with the Spirit for the kingdom to be known. (See Revelation 21; Romans 8.)

Later in the book, I will discuss the responsibility of the intercessor who is a watchman with a voice of warning. Romans 8:26 speaks of the Holy Spirit interceding for us with unspoken groanings, indicating a form of spiritual communication between God and His children. Groaning, tears, travail, and wordless prayer are forms of intercession and conversation with God in the third heaven, resulting in effective subterranean warfare.

Hypersonic Aircraft and Weapons: Worship, Gratitude, and Praise

Worship, gratitude, and praise are forms of spiritual language that express thankfulness and magnify God over all. Like a hypersonic aircraft, prophetic songs that lift our eyes to the Lord, take us to His realm, and fill our hearts with praise for Him fly past the enemy faster than the speed of sound. From here, we release hypersonic missiles that go undetected by the radar of the evil one.

Offering thanks and adoration for God's goodness, faithfulness, and mighty works delivers us from spiritual myopia. The Lord once told me that celebration is the antithesis of trauma. Trauma blocks our ability to see the blessings of the Lord, but thanking Him for our victories breaks the chokehold of pain and paves the way for freedom. Psalm 100:4 encourages us to enter His presence with thanksgiving and praise. Praise is a powerful weapon that delivers us from the bonds of despair, which come from the pressures of life and the infliction of evil. It brings healing and joy to our souls, lifting us and strengthening our faith.

Stealth Technology: Unspoken or Wordless Language

In my own words, *stealth* means to operate or hide while giving the enemy no indication as to your presence. When human words fall short, I refer to a depth of an unspoken spiritual language, which is by far the most powerful and the least detected by the enemy. Wordless conversations hold profound significance in prayer and beholding Christ, enabling believers to transcend verbal expressions and commune with God more deeply. This lack of natural language moves us from tearful intercession to shocking revelation, forms holy articulation to make accurate prophetic declarations, and breaks dependency on speaking or doing. God amplifies our connection with Him and forces us to break free from distraction, allowing us to intercede and move beyond our human understanding.

In 1 Kings 19:11–14, we see a powerful manifestation of wordless communication as a weapon of prayer. God's still, small voice spoke to Elijah, demonstrating that divine communication isn't always in physical manifestations or grandiose audible thunderings but can be in the gentlest whispers of the heart set on the Lord.

The original Hebrew word used for *small voice* is *demamah*, translated as "the voice of silence."[4] It implies an inner resounding voice within the silence and stillness, reminiscent of the "cool of the day" in Genesis 3:8, where God walked and communed with Adam and Eve amid the whispering wind of His Spirit. Thus, this connection portrays how God speaks loudly in whispers and wordless communication as we connect with Him in intimacy and vulnerability.

Embracing this spiritual language of holy breaths and silent interactions in our prayer lives empowers us to wield a powerful weapon, unlocking divine insights and facilitating a profound connection with the Almighty. We can be awestruck, finding fullness and strength as we break our need to be in control of the conversation with God and enter these wordless encounters, allowing Him to transform our prayers and forge a closer relationship between Him and us.

Friend, as we speak spiritual language, **God longs to** we are unstoppable. God answers our **take you deeper** prayers when we pray from a position **into His heart** of humility and bold confidence in His leadership. When overtaken by the Holy Spirit, we pray according to God's heart and purposes. The spirit of prophecy will come upon us to pray and speak boldly and in alignment with the truth.

These weapons in your mouth demonstrate the power and effectiveness of prayer and words when aligned with God's heart. You are invited to witness the miraculous and trust God's perfect leadership, timing, and knowledge. By abiding in Him, we align ourselves with the eternal kingdom and purpose, knowing that our days have been written in His book with divine foreknowledge.

"Out of the abundance of the heart the mouth speaks" (Matthew 12:34 ESV). God spoke the world into existence through His Word, the power of words performs intercession, and even the whisper of God is the voice of silence. Your words and prayers matter to God. What you gaze upon you will speak about and become. Look at Him and know His Word so that you will overflow with what He speaks. Get His heart on the matter, and you will see victory.

These aspects of spiritual language—the gift of tongues, prophecy, worship, praise, gratitude, tears, travails, and authoritative declarations in Jesus's name—train us to use the sword in our mouths for good and not evil.

LET'S ENCOUNTER

The Bible assures us that God answers our prayers when we are intimately in fellowship with Him, when we are silent in

His presence, and when we make authoritative declarations when we abide in Jesus (see John 15). In John 14:13–14, Jesus Himself proclaimed to His disciples, "Whatever you ask in my name, this I will do, that the Father may be glorified in the Son. If you ask me anything in my name, I will do it" (ESV). By following Jesus, we align ourselves with His authority and power so that the Son is glorified.

In this encounter, enter His identity and presence by grasping the power of His name and the power of the cross. You no longer live, but Christ lives in you as you commune with Him, and you are now to pray in His authority as an ambassador of His kingdom. In Him, tap into wisdom, revelation, and all the resources found in His blood covenant with the Father.

Knowing Him and allowing Him to search your heart thoroughly may feel uncomfortable, but He longs to take you deeper into His heart. Prepare for the Father to respond to your petition, revealing His perfect will. You are about to gain new weapons of spiritual language. Your spiritual eyes are opening, and your mouth is being consecrated. He will shape your will according to His, and you will pray, trusting in His faithfulness to accomplish what He sends forth His Word to do. Have fun in the whirlwind of surrendering to His leading; you are going to change the world.

PRAY WITH ME

Thank you, Jesus, for the power of spiritual language and the holy arsenal you have provided for me. I want you to know me, and I want to know you. Encounter me with your presence. Whether it be wordless interaction, tongues, spiritual songs, groans, shouts of gratitude, or prophetic declarations,

I invite you to come. Come now, take me into the chambers of your heart. Train me in your ways. Let me know your thoughts, and create in my mouth a holy sword. I give you my mouth and my life. Reveal your will to me. Open the scrolls of heaven, and let me read from them. I want to pray accordingly. In Jesus's name, Amen.

9

Eyes to See Beyond

Now faith is the assurance of things hoped for, the conviction of things not seen.

—Hebrews 11:1 ESV

I am fascinated by stories of history's men and women who endured persecution yet remained steadfast in faith and boldly upheld their devotion to Christ. Polycarp lived between 69 and 156 AD and was appointed bishop of Smyrna, located in modern-day Turkey, and served around fifty years. He was a mouthpiece of the Lord, and many scholars believe he was discipled by John the Beloved.[1]

In the Epistle of Polycarp to the Philippians in AD 110, he urged faithfulness in the face of persecution. Many Smyrnian believers were enduring martyrdom. Polycarp's brethren were tortured until they told of his hiding place. When the Roman soldiers arrived to arrest Polycarp, he fed them a meal and asked for an hour of prayer. They obliged. After hearing his fervent prayer, they wondered why such a godly man needed to be arrested. Therefore, they allowed one hour of intercession to become two. As I've studied God's revivalists, reformers, and martyrs, one thread is evident: They lived a lifestyle of prayer and faith.

When the eighty-six-year-old preacher walked feebly to face his accusers, the Lord spoke to him amid the shouts and jeers of an angry crowd: "Be strong and play the man."

The Roman proconsul declared to Polycarp, "I have wild animals here. I will throw you to them if you do not repent."

"Call them," Polycarp replied. "It is unthinkable for me to repent from what is good to turn to what is evil."

The proconsul then said, "If you despise the animals, I will have you burned."

Polycarp then proclaimed, "You threaten me with fire which burns for an hour, and is then extinguished, but you know nothing of the fire of the coming judgment and eternal punishment, reserved for the ungodly. Why are you waiting? Bring on whatever you want."

Finally, the proconsul said, "Take the oath [Worship Caesar and renounce Christ], and I shall release you. Curse Christ!"

Polycarp responded, "Fourscore and six years have I served him, and he has done me injury; how then can I now blaspheme my King and savior?"[2]

Tradition has it that Polycarp died by being bound and burned at the stake, then was stabbed when the fire failed to consume his body.

God had gripped Polycarp with His Spirit of Burning; he then became an eyewitness of God in his own life, a martyr who carried his testimony to the grave. He was one of those of whom "the world was not worthy" (Hebrews 11:35–40; Matthew 3:11). Polycarp knew what awaited him and faced death, knowing the promises of One who is love.[3]

The spirit of burning love and a life of intercession are more potent than any earthly flame that can kill the body. When you have become possessed by the fire of eternal love, you can feel entrapped by a body of flesh and bone. You know in your soul that death is temporary and eternal life is your reward.

The bride in Song of Solomon expresses this burning for her Bridegroom.

Set me as a seal over your heart,
 as a seal upon your arm.
For love is as strong as death,
 its jealousy as unrelenting as Sheol.
Its sparks are fiery flames,
 the fiercest blaze of all.
     —Song of Solomon 8:6 BSB

The inward branding of God is uncomfortable and often leads to earthly loss. However, heavenly realities are invaluable. People like Polycarp were not killed, but like Stephen of the Bible, they were taken up by God into glory. Long before the fire was lit to their demise, an inward holy flame consumed their souls. These would say to you that they were already dead to this world but very alive in Christ. They lived as living sacrifices and laid-down lovers.

I'll See You Soon

John the Baptist faced earthly loss. His life exemplified all three stages of becoming what Scripture describes as a faithful witness. What made John dress in camel hair and cry out in the desert instead of serving in the temple and wearing the priestly robe? He was gripped; he knew deep within what the prophets before him foresaw. Internally, he knew Jesus through the testimony of the Holy Spirit, and externally, Jesus evidently had value beyond this earth. John was an eyewitness of Jesus's works, divinity, and lifestyle; his intercession was in the wilderness cry; and he was martyred as a faithful witness who believed in the promise of Jesus.

As John blazed the trail as the one who prepared the way, all of Israel was asking one question, "Has the Messiah arrived, and is He John?" Instead of allowing himself to rise, he decreased, handed Jesus the flaming baton, and finished his race, believing in an unrealized promise.

As John faced martyrdom, he sent word to Jesus in one last wilderness cry, as if to say, "Testify to me again, Jesus. Tell me the suffering is worth it—are you the Messiah?"

> When John, who was in prison, heard about the deeds of the Messiah, he sent his disciples to ask him, "Are you the one who is to come, or should we expect someone else?"
>
> Jesus replied, "Go back and report to John what you hear and see: The blind receive sight, the lame walk, those who have leprosy are cleansed, the deaf hear, the dead are raised, and the good news is proclaimed to the poor. Blessed is anyone who does not stumble on account of me."
>
> —Matthew 11:2–6 NIV

I imagine Jesus saying it this way: "Tell John not to stumble. This is what you were born to do. You did not take the glory. You became a prophet and intercessor. Your priesthood was perfect in my sight. You decreased for my sake. You are my faithful trailblazer, and you gave up all the comforts of this world to fulfill the Father's prophecy. You have seen, heard, testified, and listened. The word of truth goes forth, and it will not return void. Those denied by the religious leaders will hear your testimony of me. It's worth it, cousin. Your blood will cry out even more than your voice in the wilderness did. Your testimony of me will never die. I am walking the same road. I'll see you soon."

If You Are Willing to Accept It

As these disciples of John were going away, Jesus began speaking to the crowds about John: "What did you go out into the wilderness to see? A reed shaken by the wind? But what did you go out to see? A man dressed in soft clothing? Those who wear soft clothing are in kings' palaces! But what did you go out to see? A prophet? Yes, I tell you, and one who is more than a prophet. This is the one about whom it is written:

'BEHOLD, I AM SENDING MY MESSENGER AHEAD OF YOU, WHO WILL PREPARE YOUR WAY BEFORE YOU.'

Truly I say to you, among those born of women there has not arisen anyone greater than John the Baptist! Yet the one who is least in the kingdom of heaven is greater than he. And from the days of John the Baptist until now the kingdom of heaven has been treated violently, and violent men take it by force. For all the Prophets and the Law prophesied until John. And if you are willing to accept it, John himself is Elijah who was to come. The one who has ears to hear, let him hear."

—Matthew 11:7–15

Some look at this passage and wonder why Jesus did not save John if He is a protector and advocate. But Jesus's answer makes me weep. He confirmed to John that He was true to His call; John, in turn, remained true to his. He upholds and validates it to those who, in weak moments, question in their hearts. Our Messiah, born of woman, demonstrates the greatness, the prophetic identity of an ordinary man during the moment of doubt. We can see God's tender character as the greatest advocate, affirmer, and protector in how He responds to John's message to Him.

A Lifestyle of Faithfulness

Josef Tson said, "Your supreme weapon is killing. My supreme weapon is dying."[4] Dying well is winning, not defeat. Many start well, but few finish well. Psalm 116:15 says, "Precious in the sight of the LORD is the death of His godly ones."

The word *witness* speaks of evangelism to most Christians. At the new birth, the inner witness is born. Many think the pinnacle is to share the Gospel with others, creating a conversion from living in sin to living as a Christian. The minimum goal is to "plant a seed," and the slam dunk is for a sinner to pray, "Jesus, come into my heart and be Lord of my life." While this is a noble act, a small margin of Christians are dedicated to being faithful witnesses of the kingdom of God, which encompasses power, authority, glory, suffering, intimacy, maturing, and unveiling unseen heavenly mysteries.

The Bible says, "It is the glory of God to conceal a matter; to search out a matter is the glory of kings" (Proverbs 25:2 NIV). We are redeemed into a heavenly priesthood and kingship, according to 1 Peter 2:9. Our job is to seek Him out and live from the overflow of what we witness—that which we see, hear, and believe by heart.

Jesus is identified as the faithful witness, and Hebrews 12:2 says Jesus is "the founder and perfecter of our faith" (ESV). He is the perfect example of a lifestyle of faithfulness to God. Further, Revelation 1:5 declares, "And from Jesus Christ, who is the faithful witness, the firstborn from the dead, and the ruler of the kings of the earth" (NIV). If Jesus is the Faithful

Witness, even unto death, even death on a cross, then He is also how we measure our faithfulness.

His zeal for us consumes Him. He runs to the fire of passion, pressure, and even persecution, not away from it. By knowing His life, we are motivated to do the same. We also get a glimpse of the glory, heavenly mysteries, and secrets as we search Him out. The mysteries and secrets disclosed to those who are willing to live faithfully will etch the testimony of the living Messiah into our DNA.

Feel the Burn

It takes stretching, pressing, and sharpening to walk holy. These characteristics of spiritual maturity are not microwavable—divine glory operates from seasons of long-suffering. In trials, we get to choose to set our gaze heavenward and remove the plank out of our eye so that later, we can compassionately remove the speck from our brother's. We don't get to whine out, tap out, or wimp out; we get to humble ourselves, go low, and build strength.

Think about getting in your spiritual squat position and going as low as possible; soon your legs begin to shake while holding that squat. All the while, your trainer won't give you an out. He says, "You can go lower and hold longer. This is building a powerhouse in you." The lower you go and the longer you wait, the more strength you build. One day, you have the mental and spiritual strength to tell your body what to do instead of it telling you.

As my friend Tom Ledbetter tells me, "The door is in the floor." In other words, the way up is down. You might want to punch your enemy in the face while you're in pain, but you will find it in yourself to have self-control, composure, and focus. It's time to toughen up, buttercup; you are a cross-carrying living sacrifice, and God is fashioning you into a faithful witness. Early Christians were ready to die for their faith; they lived contrary to the liberal politics of Rome. They had been trained to be bold and brave and even defy traditions, laws, and customs that contradicted kingdom truths or the values exemplified by Jesus.

If the church of the martyrs has one thing to teach us, it is this: The Church is the most politically potent not when she has a place in the halls of power but when she shares the testimony of Jesus, regardless of the consequences. If the Church hopes to see a new evangelization of the Western world, she must train her members to be ready to witness unto death, even when deadly threats seem a distant prospect.

Grind It Out or Give It Up

Six-time CrossFit champion Brooke Wells says, "I sacrifice a lot. The outcome will be worth it."[5] A faithful messenger of God will endure discontent between what is written and what is amiss in our world. Our identity is not found in how much we love God and how much we can do for Him; it is how much He loves us and what He has already done for us. We will faint when the heat is on because we will eventually run out of steam. The sacrifice we offer is our weakness.

Cross-training for the burning messenger is carrying our cross through the highs and the lows, in little and in plenty, through the glory and the fire. We journey with Him in different terrains of this fallen world while learning to abide in His strength. You cannot do this on your own, beloved. You don't have enough grit or affection for Him to run a supernatural race.

Overconfident passion was Peter's Achilles' heel before Acts 2. "But Peter declared, 'Even if I have to die with you,

I will never disown you.' And all the other disciples said the same" (Matthew 26:35 NIV). We know the story: When the pressure came, Peter denied Jesus.

But one of the twelve remained with Jesus all the way to the foot of the cross, John the Beloved. Interestingly, John called himself "the disciple whom Jesus loved." Was this arrogance? I'd say the opposite. John, Mary, and the mother of Jesus were found at the foot of the cross while all others ran and hid. These three had one thing in common: They were lovesick because they knew He first loved them. John didn't find confidence in his ability to prove his love for Jesus but found his reason for living in Jesus's love for him.

Being a witness means abiding in and trusting in Christ's love. The gifts of the Spirit are at best weakened by a vessel unwilling to sit with Him, listen to Him, pray with Him, and learn His ways. John the Baptist was declared by Jesus the greatest man born of a woman. He became a faithful witness, a martyr; he gave up his head. But human strength, psychological strength, failed him. The only thing that helped him press onward was the words of Jesus sent back to that dark prison cell. "Yes, John, I am who I am. My love for you is beyond your imagination" (my paraphrase).

"Multitudes, multitudes in the valley of decision! For the day of the LORD is near in the valley of decision" (Joel 3:14 NIV). Zeal for truth initially comes from the inward witness of the Holy Spirit. "And He [the Holy Spirit], when He comes, will convict the world regarding sin, righteousness, and judgment" (John 16:8, bracketed words added).

For John, the holy burden began in the womb and drove him into the wilderness. He left the comforts of the priestly life to wear camel hair, eat locusts and honey, and cry out as a prophet. People might have looked at him like he was a madman. But the Holy Spirit inside him pressed day and night. "The Messiah is here. Go and tell. Go and warn." John had an unearthly connection to the mission and was driven to accomplish it.

> Who will separate us from the love of Christ? Will tribulation, or trouble, or persecution, or famine, or nakedness, or danger, or sword? Just as it is written:
>
> "For Your sake we are killed all day long; we were regarded as sheep to be slaughtered."
>
> But in all these things we overwhelmingly conquer through Him who loved us.
>
> —Romans 8:35–37

Suchlike John, the burden of the Lord is your calling, but abiding in Him is your job description. The burden will increase as the day of His promised visitation draws near, but you are not alone. He desires us to come to Him, to stay near Him. The weight of affliction is becoming the weight of His glory.

The Horsemen Are Coming

Mental and physical toughness are important, but the cross of Golgotha stripped that away moments before our Savior gave up His Spirit. When insults and accusations come, we lean into Him, ascend to our seat, and zip our lips until He fills our mouths.

We guard our mouths because the tongue is our most powerful weapon. The issues of life flow from the heart, and your mouth speaks; guard your heart with all diligence and keep it open before the Holy Spirit (Proverbs 4:23). God is giving you your voice back, and your frustration is turning into a roar. But, beloved, we can't roar with the Lion until we understand what it is to suffer with the Lamb. Jesus is still the worthy Lamb who was slain, but he returns as the Lion.

Weeping endures for the night, but joy comes in the morning (see Psalm 30:5). What you have learned through suffering with Him allows you to roar with Him. In other words, let the Lion of Judah roar through you as you turn over weapons of flesh and trade them in for the armament of the Spirit. You are called into His throne room, where earthly trash is traded for heavenly treasures. You are growing a spine in this season to stand against the demonic powers you loathe.

A Christian with a spine is ready for anything the enemy hurls at him. This warrior does not resort to passive or aggressive tactics rooted in anger or manipulation but is a beloved messenger, deeply passionate for his Savior, who steadfastly proclaims the truth and wields spiritual weapons.

He has the patience to bow low and knows when to leap over barricades. He stands at attention and knows when to be at ease with the commander of the Lord's armies. A time is coming when, like Jeremiah, we will be tested. "If you have run with infantrymen and they have tired you out, how can you compete with horses? If you fall down in a land of peace, how will you do in the thicket by the Jordan?" (Jeremiah 12:5).

Beloved, we have been mere foot soldiers. The horses are coming. Will you be ready to run worthily?

> Then I saw when the Lamb broke one of the seven seals, and I heard one of the four living creatures saying as with a voice of thunder, "Come!" I looked, and behold, a white horse, and the one who sat on it had a bow; and a crown was given to him, and he went out conquering and to conquer.
>
> —Revelation 6:1–2

You were born at this appointed time in this generation; you have an invitation into God's strength but also His mysteries. You are a vessel of His authority. The formation of the unyielding witness has already begun in you. Take courage. You will be one counted worthy.

> When the Lamb broke the fifth seal, I saw underneath the altar the souls of those who had been killed because of the word of God, and because of the testimony which they had maintained; and they cried out with a loud voice, saying, 'How long, O Lord, holy and true, will You refrain from judging and avenging our blood on those who live on the earth?' And a white robe was given to each of them; and they were told that they were to rest for a little while longer, until the number of their fellow servants and their brothers and sisters who were to be killed even as they had been, was completed also.
>
> —Revelation 6:9–11

Unyielding witnesses of past and future ages are seen in Revelation 6 interceding for the Second Coming of Jesus, as well as receiving their robes and awaiting the day when the antichrist and the devil will be destroyed. These withstood the vengeance of Satan against God's elect. These did not recant their testimony or fear death. These will rule and reign with Jesus in the Millennium. They knew then and know now the deep love Jesus has for them.

Friend, we lose our lives to gain eternal crowns, yes, but more than that, to see Him and take on the fullness of reigning with Him as His bride. Child of God, the bride is your identity, and the priesthood is your job description (1 Peter 2). Through each fiery trial, you are gaining the strength necessary to run with the horses at the end of the age. Your voice cries out before Him with the Holy Spirit, "Prepare the way of the Lord." You have been gripped; don't turn back now.

Why Some Receive Their Sons Back and Others Don't

The faithful burning messengers go out with two words: "He's coming." Let us also shout out the two-word proclamation of His kingship: "Jesus reigns." I consider the moment of the near death of my own child and how these two raw words seemed to transform a burden of prayer for her healing into something earth-shaking. Wrapped within those two words are truths such as "Jesus, you reign over the wind and waves, over death and the grave, over time and space. Jesus, you reign!" With those two words, I proclaimed, "My weakness is your strength. Jayden's dying body is your temple. Jesus, I trust you. You reign."

On the other hand, there are those who do not recover; those who pray and do not receive back their dead. Some, like John Allen Chau, deliberately go into dark places; others, like Polycarp and John, are compelled to lay down their lives like Jesus. How do we trust what is not yet seen and reconcile the extremes of life and death in our hearts when we know Jesus is not the author of confusion, sickness, or death? We do this with the exact two words "Jesus reigns."

> Women received back their dead, raised to life again. There were others who were tortured, refusing to be released so that they might gain an even better resurrection. Some faced jeers and flogging, and even chains and imprisonment.
>
> —Hebrews 11:35–36 NIV

Hebrews 11 wrecks me. We call it the faith chapter, but most fail to grasp the thread of perseverance and intercession throughout it. It tells of those who put their faith in the Great I Am, conquered kingdoms, escaped death, and experienced miracles, and it tells of the way made for the Messiah's coming and kingdom reign. But often, we do not consider those who did not see their promise.

> Consider it pure joy, my brothers and sisters, whenever you face trials of many kinds, because you know that the testing of your faith produces perseverance. Let perseverance finish its work so that you may be mature and complete, not lacking anything.
>
> —James 1:2–4 NIV

In chapter 1, I posed this question: What would cause a twenty-six-year-old college student to become a martyr? The simplest answer is intercession and faith—unseen and unspoken. He was gripped with a level of faith that believed his blood would forever cry out for mercy for the Sentinelese people and result in them turning to Jesus. He considered it pure joy, and as we mature, so will we. If my life caused masses to abide in Him and know His face, I would also sow it.

Hebrews 11 calls John a faithful witness of whom the world was not worthy. And so it is with all those who believe yet do not see.

> They were put to death by stoning; they were sawed in two; they were killed by the sword. They went about in sheepskins and goatskins, destitute, persecuted and mistreated—*the world was not worthy of them*. They wandered in deserts and mountains, living in caves and in holes in the ground.
>
> —Hebrews 11:37–38 NIV, emphasis added

These believed in such a way that they became a seed of intercession sown into the earth, knowing that God had something better planned for us. I have felt this gripping in prayer. I've seen the creative miracles, yet I've also groaned with the Spirit, deeply lamenting for others to know there is more. The more we are filled with lovesick compassion, the more we realize to live is Christ and to die is gain, as the apostle Paul says. The lament is over the bondage and sin of those who do not know Him. People who think they are rich are starving from lacking His Word.

> These were all commended for their faith, yet none of them received what had been promised, since God had planned something better for us so that only together with us would they be made perfect.
>
> —Hebrews 11:39–40 NIV

I want you to see those who embodied the intercessions of the Lamb of God unto death and gain a new understanding of intercession as more than fervent prayer. These people are spoken of again in Revelation 12:11.

Others, like John the Beloved, continue their earthly cries before the throne, gain revelation, and demonstrate the power of the living Messiah. They must never have survivor's guilt but know the purpose is the same: Give it all away and demonstrate that Jesus reigns.

> Who through faith conquered kingdoms, administered justice, and gained what was promised; who shut the mouths of lions, quenched the fury of the flames, and escaped the edge of the sword; whose weakness was turned to strength; and who became powerful in battle and routed foreign armies.
>
> —Hebrews 11:33–34 NIV

In the gap, we groan, lament, long, and align with one longing for Him: to have His reward in us. We keep our eyes on

Jesus and know that we are surrounded by those witnesses who laid down their lives. They are cheering us on to take the baton, run our leg of the race, and keep the faith. When the gap feels like a broad chasm, we press upward, knowing Christ in us is the hope of glory.

> Therefore, since we are surrounded by such a great cloud of witnesses, let us throw off everything that hinders and the sin that so easily entangles. And let us run with perseverance the race marked out for us, fixing our eyes on Jesus, the pioneer and perfecter of faith. For the joy set before him he endured the cross, scorning its shame, and sat down at the right hand of the throne of God.
>
> —Hebrews 12:1–2 NIV

The blood cries out from the ground for justice for the faithful witnesses who went before us, but the blood of Jesus speaks a better word of mercy, so we have selfless compassion to lament with Him and endure to the end.

So even as we stand in complete faith for the miraculous, we must also be willing to see beyond the current moment or era, press toward the prize of eternity, and empower our loved ones and children to run this race for the greatest glory. In this hour, the Lord is asking us the hard questions: "If I give you your sons and daughters, will you give them back to me? Do you want more? Are you willing to lay it all down and believe for the greater glory?"

LET'S ENCOUNTER

Whether we know it or not, our spirit sees through an eternal lense, day and night, declaring one thing: "Jesus is God.

Prepare the way. He is coming. He is here." As we await the glorious day to see Him split the skies, we can cling to His promise and yield to the suffering that lasts but a moment but reaps unfathomable glory. We embody the example of Christ and those other burning ones who went before us, knowing God has called us His faithful messengers. Our time is now—let us cling to the truth of His promise and boldly remain unswayed in the face of trouble. Ask Him to unveil this revelation to you that connects history-shifting intercession and your becoming a faithful witness.

PRAY WITH ME

Dear Lord, I believe in your goodness and wait on the promises still to be seen. I confess that unmet expectations and unanswered prayers leave me in doubt, like John the Baptist. But I know you care to answer me with hope and confirmation of your kingship as you did Him. Jesus, I declare, "You reign." If I don't see my promise in my time, I know the day will come. Help me wait with hope, knowing I am in intercession for the greater glory. Open my eyes to the eternal perspective of the burden that I carry and turn it into joyful expectation. I want to be a faithful witness in life, in intercession, and even to the end of this life. I am depending on your strength when the burden gets heavy and when all that will suffice is your words and wisdom. Maranatha! Amen.

10

WAITING ON
THE WEIGHT OF GLORY

To make my weak heart strong and brave, send the fire. To live a dying world to save, send the fire. Oh, see me on Thy altar lay My life, my all, this very day; To crown the offering now, I pray: Send the fire!

—F. de L. Booth-Tucker

Jesus is not looking for downtrodden servants but for those He can call His friends, those with whom He can share His secrets. John 15:15 reads: "I no longer call you servants, because a servant does not know his master's business. Instead, I have called you friends, for everything that I learned from my Father I have made known to you" (NIV). The concept of friendship with God takes my breath away because both His friendship and rest are evidence of deliverance from orphanhood and performance. Unworthy and incapable as we are, He wants us by His side.

Be Still and Know He Is God

Rest is learned submission to the Spirit and entrance into great glory. Pause and think of who He is: the Living Word of God, the One who always was and always will be, and the perfect, holy, and unfailing friend who sticks closer than a brother. He expresses His heart's desire for our friendship. Jesus isn't looking for perfect friends, for no one is worthy to be called His equal. He adored those who hungered and thirsted through the trials yet failed in their faith when He was crucified. Embracing friendship with Jesus becomes the sacred key to the open door of Revelation 4, a divine summons, a holy invitation to witness and hear the inexpressible mysteries concealed from ordinary servants. He longs to unveil wonders to and through us, showcasing His miraculous power to those who have yet to know Him.

We understand that "blessed are those who hunger and thirst for righteousness, for they shall be filled" (Matthew 5:6 NKJV). But have we limited our hunger? What is our greatest longing? Do we long for Him and for others to know Him? Being still in His presence opens our ears to hear and broadens our heavenly vision. In the stillness, His beautiful pruning shears cut away everything that hinders love. As we sit in silence, we take on His unshakable attributes. When we pray from rest and actively silence temporal cares, the storms become still. So be still, be seated, be set firm, and be rejuvenated in Him.

We're Not Enough, but That's Okay

As friends of Jesus, we want the world to know Him in all of His glory. Friendship with Jesus leads others to the revelation of His unsearchable worth and beauty. We can't let ourselves or communities become barren. We have had an encounter, but we have not conceived. So we need the fire of God to fall on us again. The Lord wants to reveal so much more to His people, and it's as if we can't digest it yet (Hebrews 5:11–12).

Let me tell you, I felt such holy frustration with my lack and how the bride of Christ has settled for less than His everything that I would strike the altar where I knelt to pray. Maybe it's just me. But my frustration with the chasm between His desire for us and where we are has formed maturity and spiritual violence in me.

In groaning, weeping, and crying out for the fullness of His kingdom to come, I have been pressed through the eye of a needle. I've had to allow Him to strip away all of my wounding, trauma, church hurt, and religious baggage, and I've had to humble my haughty heart and get on my knees to squeeze through the narrow gate of the kingdom. "For the gate is narrow and few find it" (see Matthew 7:14).

In these groaning experiences, I've been transformed from anger at the failures of others and at their unwillingness to yield to God to realizing my own resistance to obeying Him. I wanted to violently take the kingdom *for* Him when He wanted me to humbly take it *with* Him.

In these beautiful times of groaning, outward expressions included distorted facial expressions, groans and sniffles, and massive tears. Times of holy frustration in intercession forge determination and fine-tune our spiritual hearing. He gives us His desires and allows us to enter the birthing pains. For many years, the Lord has been preparing you to hang on to the horns of the altar to bind yourself there and let His conviction overwhelm you so that you can righteously carry the burden of the Lord in your generation.

Still, I Choose You

Have you ever encountered God in the shower? Yes, I have. I told you we were going to *unveil it all* in this book. Some are appalled that I would bring this up, others are chuckling because you know what I'm talking about, and some of you need the fire of God to hit your mind right now. Nakedness has a way of attracting immorality, but *vulnerability is holy*.

When you enter the depths of intimacy with the Lord, He exposes and redeems the areas you want to hide the most. When you want to encounter Him in the Sunday worship service, He seems distant, but when you are in the shower— *boom*, there He is.

The Spirit of the Lord longs to surprise you in the most unlikely times to show you nothing is hidden from Him. He can handle your nakedness and your weakness.

My house was full. We were getting ready to go on a ministry trip to Virginia, where the Lord had been moving with power day and night. I had been invited to speak along with other emerging prophetic revivalists. With little time to spare, I jumped into the shower. To me, it felt like fifteen minutes, but two hours later, I exited the bathroom with blood vessels broken in my face. Groans emerged from the bathroom for hours. My husband was terrified to open the door and check on me because of the weighty glory and fear of the Lord radiating from the room. The kids laughed and said it sounded like the reverberations of a dying cow in the house.

The fear of the Lord came rushing into the shower where I stood. I was breathless and could not speak. My stomach clenched, my mouth opened, but no sound came out. I inwardly heard the Lord say, "Breathe!" Out came a groan (probably the dying cow sound).

I didn't care if I died. I was so awestruck by His glory and the weightiness of His presence, the burdens of the world seemed to vanish. His presence filled the room like a mighty, palpable force. My tightly closed eyes refused to open. My feeble human soul communed with His perfect Holy Spirit. In a holy moment, He lifted me in spirit, revealing visions of my destiny with Him, and a seismic awakening of the nations that would happen during my lifetime.

I couldn't help but respond with deep, fervent groans. In the depths of my being, I pleaded with Him, "Father, we are so flawed, so human. Why have you chosen me to carry your message of revival? You know I'll stumble and fall. Why place your trust in me?" It reminded me of the eloquent words of Isaiah, who said it this way, "Woe is me, for I am undone! Because I am a man of unclean lips, and I dwell in the midst of a people of unclean lips" (Isaiah 6:5 NKJV).

I had seen the holy King high and lifted up. I was in His throne room, vulnerable and unashamed. I didn't care if I died. In the midst of the encounter, He reminded me to breathe. He communicated without uttering a word, and my inner being replied in a language beyond human. Spirit to spirit, breath to breath, we connected. Much to my surprise, He laughed at my words, saying, "Woe is me . . . You know I am bound to mess this up."

He simply said, "I know, but still, I chose you."

I groaned again, awestruck. "Yes, Lord, send me!" As He embraced me, every trace of fear dissolved from my being. In an instant, I became aware that I was somehow wrapped in a towel, kneeling on the bathroom floor. I rose to my feet gradually, gazing into the mirror, bearing the marks of this profound encounter all over my face. One eye remained slightly hazy, and one ear felt as though it had popped. Yet none of it mattered. I could endure any physical deficiency as long as He remained with me.

181

I was unable to adequately express this encounter for months. I could not speak of it for hours. My face glowed, and my family knew whatever happened in that bathroom was holy. Still, I am not able to share all that He revealed in those hours. But I will say when you encounter Him in vulnerability, you will never be the same. He put the coal of the fiery altar to my heart and branded me.

Like Isaiah, I am familiar with my inability to deliver the fullness of His presence to others. I am fully aware of the impending weakness of my soul. God is looking for a bride who will not settle for nice smiles, handshakes, and Sunday morning hand claps coupled with manufactured mysteries and fog machines in the place of His glory. We must be willing to get real, weep, and say, "Woe is me, for I am a man of unclean lips, and I live among a people of unclean lips," or "Even if it kills me, show me your glory. I want to see your face."

The Weight of Our Need

Have you ever felt the overwhelming urge to, like the humble publican in the parable of the tax collector, passionately beat your chest and tear at your garments, all because you've come face-to-face with Him and your profound yearning for His boundless love, mercy, and forgiveness? His mercy is boundless, yet in those moments of self-reflection, you can't help but see the frailty within yourself and the imperfections of His Church, and you're left beautifully shattered.

R.C. Sproul said:

> There is a pattern to human responses to the presence of God in the Scripture and it seems that the more righteous the person is described, the more he trembles when he enters the immediate presence of God.

There is nothing cavalier or casual about the response of Habakkuk when he meets the holy God. . . . Where he saw all of the degradation and injustices that were sweeping across the landscape in his homeland and he was so offended by this that he went up into his watchtower and he complained against God and he said "God, you are so holy that you can't even behold iniquity. How can you stand by and let all these things come to pass?" And he says "I'm going to sit up here and I'm going to wait until God answers my question." . . . When God appeared to Habakkuk he said, "My lips quivered, my belly trembled, and rottenness entered my bones."

What happened to Job when he waited for the voice of God? And when God showed Himself to Job, Job said "I abhor myself. I repent in dust and ashes. I have spoken once, I'll speak no more. I will take my hand and put it upon my mouth." As Calvin said, "The uniform report of sacred Scripture is that every human being who ever is exposed to the holiness of God trembles in His presence."[1]

These experiences hold great value in the eyes of the Lord. When we embrace His holiness and shed our weaknesses, we can move forward with confidence. We come to understand that without Him, we are insignificant, yet He possesses the very words of life. You might be surprised by the newfound boldness that emerges in your prayers after an intense encounter with Him. As you travail, God is whispering, "At last, he's prepared to cultivate a deep friendship with me and undertake transformative work on this earth." In the fear of the Lord, we become illuminated by His glory, ever increasing in hunger, and giving birth to profound spiritual transformations.

Friends Suffering unto the Glory

Insatiable hunger draws us into profound revelations of God. Few were as hungry as Moses. He didn't care if it killed him;

he wanted to see the face of God. The closer he came to God, the closer he wanted to be. So again, it seems that death is a sensible price to pay for those who dare draw near the I AM. In the radiant glory of the Lord, we surrender our lesser desires, embracing a glorious exchange as we willingly yield our weaker dreams and limited aspirations, embracing fleshly defeat to gain His eternal vision and everlasting love. His goodness and love cast out all fear, even fear of death. God has fashioned us to hunger like Moses.

> Then Moses said, "Now show me your glory."
>
> And the LORD said, "I will cause all my goodness to pass in front of you, and I will proclaim my name, the LORD, in your presence. I will have mercy on whom I will have mercy, and I will have compassion on whom I will have compassion. But," he said, "you cannot see my face, for no one may see me and live."
>
> —Exodus 33:18–20 NIV

We must wholeheartedly surrender to God, aligning our prayers with His. As we surrender, we grow expectant, ready to patiently bear the weight of His presence. We recognize Him as the prize, and the pleasures of this world cannot compare to the reward of His glory. Just as God drew Moses near in a friendship that abolished fear and kindled longing, we, too, can draw nearer to God's glory. Moses's yearning resulted in the revelation of God's blueprint for establishing His kingdom on earth as it is in heaven. Moses was deeply moved by love. And that same glory awaits us.

> Then the LORD said, "There is a place near me where you may stand on a rock. When my glory passes by, I will put you in

184

a cleft in the rock and cover you with my hand until I have passed by. Then I will remove my hand and you will see my back; but my face must not be seen."

—Exodus 33:21–23 NIV

Access Granted

Moses experienced a level of God's splendor that's beyond our current comprehension, and yet, there's even greater glory available to us. This brings to mind the teachings in 2 Corinthians 3:7–13.

Paul refers to Moses's glory as *transitory, fleeting,* and *lesser* because of the ministry of condemnation. He urges us to know that we have access to an unfathomable, untold, inextinguishable, surpassing glory in the ministry of righteousness.

Now if the ministry of death, which was engraved in letters on stone, came with such glory that the Israelites could not gaze at the face of Moses because of its fleeting glory, will not the ministry of the Spirit be even more glorious? For if the ministry of condemnation was glorious, how much more glorious is the ministry of righteousness! Indeed, what was once glorious has no glory now in comparison to the glory that surpasses it. For if what was fading away came with glory, how much greater is the glory of that which endures!

Therefore, since we have such a hope, we are very bold. We are not like Moses, who would put a veil over his face to keep the Israelites from gazing at the end of what was fading away.

—2 Corinthians 3:7–13 BSB

Because of the cross, we have been transformed and transitioned into an era of grandeur and majesty. Through the blood of Christ, we can access greater glory, surpassing Moses's experience, by cultivating a lifestyle of hunger and seeking a deep friendship with God.

Conception, Birth, and Perfect Leadership

Hunger, friendship, and glory are pleasing, but they should always lead to fruitfulness. Moses was met by God because God loved him, and the encounters molded Moses into a leader who never wanted to be separated from Him. God never intended to send Moses to the promised land without Him. He wanted Moses to ask for more than just strategy and leadership; He wanted Moses to know Him and learn His ways. God was mentoring Moses to lead like Him. God spoke to Moses face-to-face as a man speaks to a friend.

Moses had to grow beyond actions like striking the rock and breaking the tablets. When the people needed water again, he was directed to speak to the rock rather than strike it. In this new era, those seeking reform should release the bitterness of the past and embrace the authority, rest, and peace available to us from our heavenly stance of intercession and declaration. Failing to do so will leave us ill prepared to lead in the promised land.

The blood of Christ and the glory of God are here to shatter the chains of spiritual slavery, freeing us for unbroken communion with Him. Our transformation reflects what we focus on; He changes us as we keep our eyes on Him and commit wholeheartedly. Our zeal for His kingdom remains unwavering, but it must be guided by the grand promise of glory.

It's time to let go of any entitlement and stop resorting to worldly weapons when facing thoughtless provocations on social media. Instead, we're called to ascend the hill of the Lord, calm our restless souls, and put our trust solely in Him. As we eagerly await His voice, we release His message with deep authority. In doing so, we effectively break down the strongholds of idolatry and rebuild with the unshakable foundation of truth. We mend shattered hearts and liberate the captives.

> Now the Lord is the Spirit, and where the Spirit of the Lord is, there is freedom. And we, who with unveiled faces all reflect the glory of the Lord, are being transformed into His image with intensifying glory, which comes from the Lord, who is the Spirit.
>
> —2 Corinthians 3:17–18 BSB

By disciplining our souls to be still, we learn to speak when He commands and to stay silent when our inner conviction suggests it. This is how we live in the greater glory as anointed intercessors and reformers.

All Eyes on the Unseen Glory

Affliction is inevitable, but we center our gaze on the face of Jesus. It is important to anchor our zeal in the promise of ultimate glory. In our fervent intercession, we intimately experience the pains of affliction and align with the profound depths of suffering for Christ. Therefore, let's take a deep breath and direct our attention to the countenance of Jesus. Our utterances and unwavering grit are being consecrated and positioned to usher forth His glorious end-time work.

In 2 Corinthians 4:17–18, Paul speaks to us about affliction and how to rise above. "For our light and momentary affliction is producing for us an eternal glory far beyond comparison. So we fix our eyes not on what is seen, but on what is unseen. For what is seen is temporary, but what is unseen is eternal" (BSB). Consider these statements specifically: "light and momentary affliction," "producing . . . eternal glory," "fix our eyes . . . on what is unseen." The statements you choose to concentrate on and the questions you pose hold significance. Engaging in a dialogue with the Lord, particularly about His Word, is a type of prayer that He truly cherishes.

The statements emphasized earlier stir my heart and ignite a growing hunger within me. A vital aspect of building faith involves taking moments when reading the Word to consider phrases like "fix your eyes on what is unseen." Start by asking yourself, "Am I too focused on what's right in front of me, on my daily challenges?" Then, approach Him with simplicity and ask, "Can you show me the eternal glory that's being formed in the things I can't see but should focus on?"

As you engage with God this way, you will start to sense a growing wonder within your spirit. Your focus is shifting from the temporary to the eternal realm.

People like Joan of Arc lived in infinite wonder as they became unyielding in their lifestyle as the Lord's witnesses. *Whether you have been saved for four days or forty years, the trials of your journey with Christ have begun to build your personal history with Him.* He is sure of His faithfulness, but He proves His ways are higher, better, and more enjoyable than anything the world offers.

The more history we build with Him, the more we become deeply acquainted with His ways, rewards, and even sufferings. Consider the setbacks, failures, sin patterns, and hopeless cycles you have overcome with Him. How often do you weep in prayer or intercession, not see an immediate change in the circumstance, but get up feeling hopeful, loved, and refreshed by His presence? That's because you know you can anticipate the glory that is to come.

Friend, you have spent years building your personal history with God:

- through the inner darkness of being misunderstood
- in feeling unseen by man but totally known by God
- in the glory days of enjoying favor and increasingly knowing it was by His hand
- in feeling His quiet nearness and intense interventions
- in walking in realms of divine revelation of His Word
- through victories, miracles, and healings occurring at times that would have otherwise been fatal to your soul
- through these trials, you have blazed trails for others to follow

When we fix our eyes on what is unseen, we emanate hope. As we continue this journey of awakening the groan, we will become more equipped to articulate the blueprints of heaven and build a dwelling place for revival in our sphere of influence. Our home of power is in the heavenly realms. Once we practice abiding with Him in holy places and work from our scriptural position, God opens doors for us to manifest His glory on earth, doors that will never be closed. Remember, Revelation 3:7 says that Jesus is the one "who opens and no one will shut, who shuts and no one opens" (ESV).

The journey, which requires patience, that we are taking together in this book of encounters, revelations, prayers, and teachings will settle our anxious souls and release the unseen wonder written in Scripture through us. Our calling and commissioning as friends and children of God is to sit with Him, wait in Him, and move in sync with Him. We get to wait on the weight of His glory to come on and through us. Let's keep our eyes locked on Jesus and ask Him to take us up and reveal His unshakable kingdom. He's calling us higher in this hour like no other generation before us. Will you follow His lead?

And the voice I had first heard speaking to me like a trumpet said, "Come up here, and I will show you what must take place after this." At once I was in the Spirit, and there before me was a throne in heaven and someone sitting on it.

—Revelation 4:1–2 NIV

Beloved, I declare this to you: Your face is unveiled. Release the weight of this world and its suffering as you wait on His glory. You have been through the fire, and it is time to reflect on God's unceasing glory. Your cry will be like Moses's: "Unless you go with me, I don't want to go." It is time for freedom to burn in His glory more intensely than Moses experienced. You are a glory carrier, learning to live *for* Him, *from* Him, and *in* Him. You are becoming a faithful witness.

LET'S ENCOUNTER

He's calling you and a remnant of sacred voices to come. Inwardly, your spirit groans in reply, "Yes, I want nothing more than to come." In this activation, silence everything else in the room. Turn off your phone for five minutes. Then, ask Him aloud to reveal to you the throne and the place where you have been invited to sit.

Close your eyes, and with your sanctified imagination, see Him according to His Word. See His eyes like fire, hair like wool, and realize you have full access to Him, face-to-face, because of His blood. Wait on Him. Let the silence penetrate the chatter of your soul. Wait on the weight of His glory. Draw near. Ask for more amid the intensity. Enter the throne room and enjoy His presence.

Pause. Look at Him with your spiritual eyes. See His delight in you. Oh, He has longed for you to come and learn to abide with Him. Now ask for Him to unveil His will for your life. Then, ask for it to be done on earth as it is written in His holy book. Ask Him to awaken the groan of intercession for "His kingdom to come on earth as it is in heaven." Ask Him for increased discernment and holy grit to tarry with Him in this hour.

Be still for a few more moments; linger in this place. Take just thirty seconds to jot down your questions for Him and what He spoke to you. Practice this daily and watch Him increase your awareness of His presence.

PRAY WITH ME

Dear God, help me understand this groan of the Spirit in me. As I am still and wait on you, I want my heart to burn uncontrollably and to no longer regard this life as anything compared to my eternal home in you. Teach me to wait on the weight of your glory. Amen.

11

THE REWARD
OF TOTAL SURRENDER

Father, if thou be willing, remove this cup from me: never-theless not my will, but thine, be done.

—Luke 22:42 KJV

In chapter 1, I described how the Lord stole me away to Israel, practically packing my bags and taking me to His homeland. I thought I was going on a mission trip to reach others, but I was being captivated. In the Garden of Gethsemane, Jesus called me to Himself and offered the treasure of His mysteries through the sweet whispers of His heart: "Tammie, do you want more?"

Given the setting, I knew He was inviting me into His suf-ferings and His intercessions, but the reward would be *more of Him*. At that time, I was well-acquainted with the grief of following His Spirit; my voice shook with hesitation at the high cost to take hold of the *more* He was presenting. Over the next twenty-four hours, I experienced Jesus's voice and presence with increasing intensity. From Gethsemane to His prison cell, with an eye-to-eye open vision, again He said, "Tammie, do you want more?"

He looked into my eyes. His face was covered in blood, and His head crowned with thorns in the pit where He was held the night before His crucifixion. He then said, "I could have left this pit at any moment, but I surrendered my life in the garden of travail hours before they confined me here when I agreed with the Father's way, 'Not my will but Thine be done.'"

Will You Tarry with Him?

Many see His sacrifice on the cross and think that is where Jesus gave His life, but actually it's where He made His intercession public; He chose to die long before Golgotha. He's the Lamb that was slain before the foundation of the earth. The cross, His blood, and His suffering were the public platform of His grand intercession for all of humanity. In my garden encounter, He offered me a trade, my life for His, my prayers for His, my platform for His. In my search for the mysteries and treasures of heaven, and in my cries for the next great awakening, would I relinquish all my earthly dreams to glorify Him, to purchase His field, which contained pearls of great value?

> Again, the kingdom of heaven is like treasure hidden in a field, which a man found and hid; and for joy over it he goes and sells all that he has and buys that field.
>
> —Matthew 13:44 NKJV

He was not giving me an invitation to gain more fortune, fame, or favor with man. These things are not bad or good;

they can be used to further the kingdom, but there is more. Our lamenting God asked me a question similar to what He asked His friends the night they dozed on their watch. Did I want more than great clout or a mighty ministry? What if my platform looked like His, a cross of groaning intercession and bearing the weight of His burden for human redemption? Was I willing to trade my lifelong dreams to tarry with Him in this modern hour of crisis?

He's also asking you: Do you want to enter the revelations of His sufferings, the unveilings of His mysteries, the formation of His glory in you? Are you willing to pay the price? Beloved, are we willing to groan with Him in this hour when many will fall asleep, become disillusioned, or even betray Him? What if it doesn't look like you thought? What are you willing to sacrifice for the great anointing you carry?

He's weeping. Will you weep with Him? Will you stay awake through the intensity? Will you cash in your spiritual nest egg to spend your days mining for pearls in His garden? This is the hour of great mystery and lament, and you are invited to the watch party as a watchman on the wall.

A Little Disclosure

This chapter will demand our capability to take Israel's warnings and judgments as prophetic and apply them to ourselves and the present-day Christian culture. It's crucial to glean wisdom from their mistakes and heed Jesus's call to the modern Church era. We represent today's religious culture, preparing for His return. However, we might find ourselves entrenched in our established ministerial customs, possibly inclined to compromise to align with the prevailing political climate. Could the Gentile church become blinded in the hour of His visitation?

Perhaps you recognize the entitled, wayward disaster Christendom has entered. Many of you grieve and yearn for Him to come with revival and awakening. The unspoken heavenly appeal keeps you up at night. Jesus is zealous for His bride to carry His zeal and provoke the Jews to jealousy. But did you consider the moments of tears as divine in exchange for His heart and intercessions for those who defame His name? His anointing and presence will accompany you with power, but prepare to hold your plans lightly in the coming season of reformation. Remember that He died not to elevate us but to give us His face—there is *more*.

The Secrets of the Garden Are Yours

God paints interesting prophetic pictures. He's a hopeless romantic but an unrelenting Savior. He laughs, cries, suffers, fights with the breath of His mouth, and always wins. The prophetic expression of redemption began in the Garden of Eden and peaked in the Garden of Gethsemane so that He could restore us to be His garden, unlocked forever. His desire was never to be without us but to be *one with us*.

Friend, you are more than your gift. He's not as interested in *using you* as He is in *being with you*. You are more than an intercessor, prophet, teacher, pastor, or even student, mom, or dad to Him. There are mysteries to be opened, some buried deep within you that will only be discovered as you unrelentingly pursue knowing Him. The garden unveils secrets while you take advantage of liberation to commune with Him where human language fails. In the garden, you rule and reign with Him forever. You and I have the opportunity to journey with Him through the way of His intercessory sufferings in the corridor of His glory.

There is *more*.

Jesus Laments

The lament of Jesus is a phenomenon. This weeping Man is God embodied and knows the end from the beginning. He is not anxious or fearful of the outcome. Yet He weeps. He groans and asks His friends to grieve with Him. When you are His friend, He attracts you to what grieves Him and to what brings Him joy. "Then He said to them, 'My soul is deeply grieved, to the point of death; remain here and keep watch with Me'" (Matthew 26:38).

My encounter with Him began in the garden that day, but what happened over the next few hours, days, and years shook me to my core. He invited me to a profound friendship with Him, and I gave Him a weak yes. Daily, He still asks me, "Tammie, *do you want more?*"

One of the most critical hours of intercession ever recorded is in the Garden of Gethsemane. (It is second only to the moment He cried out on the cross, "Father, forgive them, for they know not what they do," and gave up His spirit.) In the garden, the night before His crucifixion, He sweated blood while He wailed. The cup of sorrow was placed before Him. Was His distress due to the fear of the pain He was about to go through? Might it be, at least partly, that He knew that the unfolding events would further harden Israel's heart? Was He in anguish over the rejection by Abraham's seed as He redeemed humanity?

Jesus knew that the sacrifice of His life would bring salvation to everyone who repents and receives. Perhaps Judas represented all those in Israel and in future Christianity who would cast Him away with obstinate hearts. Judas betrayed Him to fulfill the prophecy, and many more Jews would follow. Zoom out for a moment and apply Israel's blindness to modern Christianity. Do you think Jesus saw our hardness and apostasy before His Second Coming (see 2 Thessalonians 2:10)? His tears always mean more than what we see.

Judas, the son of perdition, is a small prophetic snapshot of the man of lawlessness, the Antichrist, who will rise up to deceive the whole world at the end of the age before Christ's return. In context, John 17:12 refers to Judas Iscariot; and 2 Thessalonians 2:3 refers to the Antichrist.

We see the scenery and the context of Jesus's travail moments before Judas betrays Him with a kiss. The answers to these questions could help us better understand why the Son of God was so vexed, why He asked His friends to tarry with Him and grasp the anguish woven in the Holy Spirit's groan within us in this age (Matthew 26:40; Luke 22:44; Romans 8:26).

Could He have felt the weight of the mission on His heart, including the cup coming to Israel? Our Savior is relentless! The world's weight was truly on His shoulders. Was He deeply vexed by the consequences of sin, judgment, and the shaking necessary for the birth of righteousness in His beloved people, yet full of joy as He endured the cross for you and me? He had much weighing on Him during that hour, and it was more than concern about how He would face the coming pain. His intercession would move beyond a guttural groan into a death, etching into eternity the way of redemption and sealed with His blood. It was the only way to complete the transition from the age of fading glory to the age of eternal majesty.

Jesus Groans over Jerusalem

"Jerusalem, Jerusalem, who kills the prophets and stones those who have been sent to her! How often I wanted to gather your children together, the way a hen gathers her chicks under her wings, and you were unwilling. Behold, your house is being left to you desolate! For I say to you, from now on you

198

will not see Me until you say, 'BLESSED IS THE ONE WHO COMES IN THE NAME OF THE LORD!'"

—Matthew 23:37–39

The Pharisees were the leaders of the Jewish people, but the spirit of religion hardened their hearts. They functioned more as politicians than as lovers of God. They used the words of the prophets to further their political agenda and talked of the Messiah coming to benefit their power positions. They told the people He would make everything right with a sword and conquer Rome. But when He came lowly and demonstrated the kingdom, He was a threat to their platforms, systems, and control of the people. They rejected Him and those who believed in Him.

This is the religious spirit at its finest. It is double-minded, self-serving, controlling, and often political. Jesus prophesied that the people of Jerusalem would bless Him and some would acknowledge His Messiahship, but soon after, they would destroy Him (see John 2:19). He would rise again, but their rejection of Him would reap desolation (see Luke 19:44).

And as soon as He was approaching, near the descent of the Mount of Olives, the whole crowd of the disciples began to praise God joyfully with a loud voice for all the miracles which they had seen, shouting:

"BLESSED IS THE KING, THE ONE WHO COMES IN THE NAME OF THE LORD; PEACE IN HEAVEN AND GLORY IN THE HIGHEST!"

And yet some of the Pharisees in the crowd said to Him, "Teacher, rebuke Your disciples!" Jesus replied, "I tell you, if these stop speaking, the stones will cry out!"

—Luke 19:37–40

Does any of this sound familiar? Jesus's time with them was drawing to a close. His tears of intercession turned to words of warning. He walked among them and established the kingdom of heaven. Though He knew He would come again, He urgently warned of their blindness, hardness of heart, and rejection of the prophets and prophesied that soon they would hunt down and kill the voices sent to them. Beloved, we are also to heed His warning.

> When He approached Jerusalem, He saw the city and wept over it, saying, "If you had known on this day, even you, the conditions for peace! But now they have been hidden from your eyes. For the days will come upon you when your enemies will put up a barricade against you, and surround you and hem you in on every side, and they will level you to the ground, and throw down your children within you, and they will not leave in you one stone upon another, because you did not recognize the time of your visitation."
>
> —Luke 19:41–44

Oh, that we would know the time of our visitation. This makes me weep. It causes supplication to stir in me for the modern-day Church. As we grow in understanding of the burden of the Lord in prayer, let us also see how history prophesies with alarm about times to come. Will we, too, become blind?

He longed to gather them to Himself and still does, and He will before He comes again. Their eyes had become blind and their ears deafened to His voice. Using the Scriptures, they overemphasized the letter of the law and became blind guides (Matthew 15:14). He wept intensely over the destruction that would come because they had chosen power over promise. The one they cried out for was among them, but He did not lead politically or with an iron fist. He administered justice to the weak, marginalized, abused, and rejected of Israel.

For Jesus, the zeal for His house is consuming (John 2:17), but He longs to gather the religious under the shelter of His wings (Matthew 23:27). Jesus knows His war is not against flesh and blood but against unseen spiritual wickedness (Luke 19:41–44). He wants you and me to move when we hear His voice and abide so close to His heart that we provoke others to return to Him. We must not shrink back when intimidation comes but bury ourselves deeper into Him.

Identifying with His Sufferings

Our intercession has prophetic layers. I have wept, paced the floor, and fasted for my children and the Church to be free from this age's influence. It seems like hell itself is in our children's faces day and night. I have knocked on the doors of heaven, asking and seeking answers so these young ones would not be lost to the world's deception. I am sure you have as well. The Holy Spirit's lament in us is too deep for words. Friend, as we understand this kind of intercession for our children, we must also be gripped for the sleeping Church. We can zoom out the lens and consider the sorrow of our Savior as He laid down His life.

Jesus's groan was intense; He did not weep pretty little prayers but cried out in the garden to restore us to be His fruitful garden, a dwelling place for Him. He longs to gather His children and His bride with greater intensity than we do. He wants us delivered from the antichrist agenda of sexual sin, pride, perversion, political idolatry, self-worship, wars, murders, and eternal death. He now invites us as His friends into groaning. We must cry out for the Church and her people to wake up from slumber, cease rebellion, and recognize and enjoy His visitation day.

Nazirites and Prophets Come Alive

Many anointed voices, prophets, and consecrated messengers have risen among the redeemed throughout history. Unlike Israel, God has given us His Spirit and taught us by His Scriptures that gifts of the Spirit are given to build up the Church. We are without excuse. The bride of Christ is experiencing defilement, slumber, barrenness, and miscarriages. Cancel culture and woke culture have crept into our board and planning meetings, threatening to render the Church impotent. Due to the fear of man and political pressure, we are silencing the true prophets and telling the consecrated ones to throttle their fire and drink the secular wine.

We often talk about Amos 9:11, the rebuilding of David's fallen tent, and being modern-day Levites. Still, we have watered down so much of the power of the Gospel that we need the rebuke of Amos 2:11–12 before we can ever experience the bliss of Amos 9:11. We must heed a strong warning and wake-up call.

> "I also raised up prophets from among your children and Nazirites from among your youths. Is this not true, people of Israel?" declares the LORD. "But you made the Nazirites drink wine and commanded the prophets not to prophesy."
>
> —Amos 2:11–12 NIV

The call to intercession isn't simply an invitation to pray. It is about becoming a fearless watchman who worships and declares truth in the ears of those who will probably reject the Lord's Word. Jesus is the spirit of prophecy and the spirit of prayer; when we pray, we embody His mission. He weeps, laments, mourns, prophesies, leads, and performs judgment and justice. He also gathers, protects, delivers, heals, and restores us to purity and Himself. His laments went forth in the Garden of Gethsemane, groans for Israel and for us, and His blood continues interceding for us day and night, calling us to walk in our spiritual inheritance. He gave His life to restore us to Eden.

Open Your Mouth

We must break free of the fear of man and open our mouths, no matter the cost. The Lord has been preparing the Church for His Second Coming through wordless encounters, intercession, prophecy, and the resurgence of fivefold gifts. But ministry gifts, such as prophecy, apostleship, and evangelism, have been either worshiped and politicized or stifled, oppressed, and rejected.

The stifling happened in an attempt to mature and bring purification to prophetic voices. Unfortunately, we overcorrected and taught true burden bearers to only pray the Word of the Lord and not prophesy without the approval of a committee. While well-meaning and somewhat effective, this safeguard often overstays its welcome, leading to the prolonged silencing of mature prophets and the hyping of organizational positions, perpetuating the orphan mentality. As the gift matures, instead of being honored, the person second-guesses their ability to hear God or develops approval addiction or codependency. Even worse, the gift becomes dormant as the person honors man over the voice of the Lord. The Lord is exposing and correcting, saying, "Let my prophets intercede, let them speak."

If you feel the sting of these statements, either you have been stifled or you have overcorrected others due to your burden

203

for the purification of the prophetic movement. The Father has seen the silent suffering of the pure in heart. Be encouraged, there is purpose in the pressure. Those unwilling to take on fame or who submitted to overcorrecting leadership as unto the Lord were purposefully bent in the wilderness season, one of uncomfortable weeping and groaning. His grace is sufficient to bring deliverance from the fear of man and awaken the mature gift in you again. Leaders who overcompensated with pure intentions probably did so because it was done to them.

Leader, He is healing your heart, is preparing you to be a deliverer, and will use you to unleash a roar in this generation. It will get messy, but as He did with Israel, He desires to gather His Church for the day of His visitation. His faithful ministry must move into alignment and begin to tear down, rebuild, cry out for mercy, and sound the alarm of His coming. If not, like the religious of old, the elect may even be deceived (see Matthew 24:24).

The Watchman's Duty

Many intercessors have been taught that groaning, tears, and travail are simply their sole occupation in the body of Christ. That is not entirely true. Though the cross is your platform, you don't get a free pass when it comes to the Great Commission. His chosen messengers have agreed to bear with Him in longsuffering. This is kind of a big deal. He wants you to know that you are precious and influential in the hidden place as an intercessor, but you are more than a prayer warrior. You are His garden, where He brings forth His spiritual fruit, and you are His mouthpiece, first in the heavenly realm and then in the earth.

Ezekiel 33 states the watchman's duty to pray and sound the warning alarm.

But if the watchman sees the sword coming and does not blow the trumpet to warn the people and the sword comes and takes someone's life, that person's life will be taken because of their sin, but I will hold the watchman accountable for their blood.

—Ezekiel 33:6 NIV

Perhaps you have been led to believe that what you see, hear, and encounter is reserved only for hidden places of prayer, not to be spoken before man. The Lord says, "Those who have locked themselves in my inner chambers will emerge with purity and power. Their season of hiddenness has delivered them from the praise of man and allowed them to lean into zeal for my house. They will always desire the hidden place alone with me, even when they minister before man. I am healing them and setting them free from approval addiction that resulted from overcorrection."

Beloved, out of the abundance of the heart, the mouth speaks. He longs to break the seal that has locked you into a label and open a fountain of truth to spring forth. "You are a garden locked up, my sister, my bride; you are a spring enclosed, a sealed fountain" (Song of Solomon 4:12 NIV).

Many hidden intercessors are about to burst forth from prayer rooms and closets with the power of demonstration; you are one of this company and an alarm in the earth. Your life will declare that the kingdom of heaven is at hand. You will be faithful with the word you carry; you have learned to take it to the throne before you take it to man's ears.

Friend, you are His garden, and the brightness of His light within you reveals the urgency of the hour. You have mourned with Him in prayer and lived in fellowship with His Church, even when she shut down His voice. The pressure of the hidden season has developed tenderness of heart. Our Bridegroom's intense weeping for Jerusalem deepened as He lived among them because He humbled Himself to visit their families and teach in their synagogues. You have learned to love like Him. Now you can speak with the tenderness of His voice.

God leads us into regions, ministries, communities, and churches to bear the burden for them with Him. He asks many to build a bridge in apostolic intercession between the local church, the house of prayer, and the house church movements. We are not sent to agree with the enemy's accusations or to divide but to intercede for a move of reconciliation and great glory.

The time will come when the mercy will run out for any religious structure that engages in pharisaical or antichrist cultural ideologies, like those involved in the ways of Babylon. Babylon is called a harlot because she has a form of religion but denies consecration and holiness to Yahweh alone. Babylon is full of worldly seduction and leads the kings of the earth astray with her immoralities.

As stated in Revelation 17:2, the spirit of Babylon is the one "with whom the kings of the earth have committed fornication, and the inhabitants of the earth were made drunk with the wine of her fornication" (NKJV). Though we intercede, we must also *come out from among this mixture*. We carry the heart and burden of the Lord and sound the alarm in prayer, compassion, and humility seasoned with holy tears and fear of the Lord.

Releasing Our Burdens to Open the Gate

Intercessors and leaders in the body of Christ, perhaps you have felt stripped down, unable to go forward, and like you are at an impasse. Perhaps you have felt you cannot climb over the wall in front of you. While you may have felt you were at an impasse, I invite you to consider that perhaps you are at a closed gate that only opens for the King of Glory.

The LORD said to me, "This gate is to remain shut. It must not be opened; no one may enter through it. It is to remain shut because the LORD, the God of Israel, has entered through it. The prince himself is the only one who may sit inside the gateway to eat in the presence of the LORD."

—Ezekiel 44:2–3 NIV, emphasis added

The One who can enter through the gate is the Ancient of Days; therefore, Psalm 24 is the prescription. You must ascend the hill of the Lord with clean hands and a pure heart. Bow low, but lift up your head that the King of Glory may come in.

Somewhere between asleep and awake, I had a dream-like encounter; I call these experiences *drisions* or "dream-visions." I saw the rooms and doors of heaven. The Lord was unfolding the depths of His abode. As I moved through the open doors of heaven, I noticed that they were circular, portal-shaped doors, not vertical. These doors open through the revelation of Jesus as the sacrificial Lamb.

I knew the blood of the Lamb was the gateway. The Lamb, as declared in Revelation 13:8, was *slain before the foundation of the earth*; He is the Ancient Gate and the Ancient Pathway. Therefore, these gates and pathways are older than we thought—maybe eternal? I heard a trumpet or a voice quoting Psalm 24, "Lift up your heads, you gates, and be lifted up, you ancient doors." The heads of the leaders of the earth were lifted up to see Him; suddenly, the doors from heaven to earth opened. The leaders of the earth were simultaneously humbled by the fear and awesomeness of the Lord as they beheld Jesus.

From that place of humility and fear of the Lord, the earthen doors were opened so that the Ancient of Days could enter our era. Jesus, the Lamb, held blueprints and scrolls that were written before time began. It was as if He were waiting on the earth to bow low and look to Him for help.

In the dream-like encounter, I felt divine emphasis on the ancient pathways and a warning for the modern Church to repent of following after the mixture of our age. Like John in Revelation 4, He was calling, "Come up here" and come through the revelation of the Lamb to "ancient pathways." As the heads of the kings of the earth lift to behold the King of glory, He enters and opens the path to righteousness and gives us great depths of intercession and revelation. He reveals His kingdom and leads us into paths of righteousness for His namesake.

This encounter reminds us of Jacob's ladder in Genesis 28:12. Here, the Lamb acts as the ladder, the sons and daughters of God serve as intercessors who ascend and descend as messengers of the age, and the gateway is opened for the kings of the earth to humbly bow and gaze upon the King of Glory. He unveils His scrolls, opens His doors, and grants access to His gates to those who are willing to look beyond earthly strife and trust in the unseen heavenly strategy to establish His way in this era. However, we must first be willing to let Him deliver us from the ways of Babylon and humble ourselves.

Matthew 19:24 says, "Again I tell you, it is easier for a camel to go through the eye of a needle than for someone who is rich to enter the kingdom of God" (NIV). We are being pressed through the "eye of the needle" in this era. This means that we will need to dismount from what we've been driving, or rather, what has been driving us. We must also shed all baggage, burdens, and unscriptural ideologies if we aim to pass through the gate with the King. We must return to the eternal foundations of the faith, as these ancient paths take us to the opening of ancient gates.

In order to enter the gate of the city of the Lord, we must be stripped down and unhindered by manufactured systems or the fear of man. This obedience will open the door. This stripping away is very personal and intimate. Those who go with you must follow the same process.

The people of God must again become responsible for their families, maturity, and growth. No longer will the Lord allow ministers to carry the unhealthy burden of all the people, but once pastors and ministers have given Him these burdens, they will become shepherds after His heart, leading others into paths of righteousness. All must apply salvation to their lives and grow up in Him. The people of God will get delivered from a milk-based diet and begin to feast on the meaty revelation within the Word of God.

The family table is being restored as you enter through the eye of the needle. Minister, your leadership will be more valuable, restful, and powerful to the people after you submit to this offloading process. You are being set free from false responsibilities—in this, you and your family will be restored. Celebrate this season of stripping away the old in preparation for entering the new. Release the burdens. Go low and welcome the King of Glory as He walks through the gate once sealed shut.

Tables, Tabernacles, and Platforms

The next significant move of God will center around *tables* as we become His dwelling place or tabernacle; elevated *platforms* will be humbled. In Scripture, the table is an iconic place of feasting on the presence of God, priesthood, and consecration. In the Holy Place, there were three pieces of furniture all made of pure gold: the lampstand, the altar of incense, and the table of shewbread. Twelve loaves of shewbread, also called the bread of His face or bread of the presence, were made of the purest ingredients and sat in the Holy Place for seven days. On the Sabbath, the priest would eat it. Thus, God and man would share the table, fellowship, and bread together.

In the New Testament, Christ broke bread and ate it in fellowship with His friends (1 Corinthians 10:16–21). He also stated, "Man shall not live on bread alone, but on every word that comes from the mouth of God" (Matthew 4:4 NIV) when Satan tempted Him to turn the stones into bread. The bread and the table represent priestly fellowship, holy transformation, and abiding in the One who is the bread together. Jesus also flips the tables in the temple when they are misused, saying, "My house shall be called a house of prayer for all nations, not a den of thieves and robbers" (Matthew 21:13, author's paraphrase).

The golden table, the bread, the lampstand, and the incense of intercession signify face-to-face fellowship between God and man in prayer and praise. As stated in 1 Corinthians 3:16, He has called us His temple, and is restoring us to the table where we can enter beyond the veil together. Meetings will become thicker with glory when the table comes into play. No matter how powerful a conference or large meeting is, it can only be a small part of transformation over the long haul.

Jesus's revolution will prioritize relational authenticity over spotlight and fame. He will clear our transactional tables from selling the Holy Spirit's gifts and flip them to places of communion and transfiguration, mirroring the profound meeting of Moses, Elijah, and Jesus on the Mount of Transfiguration in Matthew 17:1–8. In Acts, they met in the temple courts, broke bread in their homes, and were transformed as they lived life together in His presence. This transformation resulted in thousands being added to their number daily. Small meetings sustained them, but larger gatherings, such as the feasts, provoked and galvanized them.

Our man-made platforms create an opportunity for the masses to encounter God together if done in purity, but at most, they are outer-court experiences. I love a stadium full of worshipers and intercession. The Lord allows us to grow powerfully in Him together through conferences and tent gatherings. Yet it all loses its purpose if leaders aren't leading lives of intercession and if the attendees aren't being transformed into His image, praying, worshiping, and demonstrating love for one another in their homes and in daily life.

We can't live on bread alone. We need open hands and hearts. We must daily feast on every word while being seated in fellowship with Him in His presence. We must become His tabernacle and be transformed at His table. He loves to bless us with His glory. When we've each cultivated the garden of our hearts in small and secret ways, we will enjoy feasting on His glory together. Who knows, maybe He will add three thousand to our number daily.

The Reward of Total Surrender

Just as the Lord of angel armies guided the Israelites through circumcision before they entered the promised land, today He is guiding us to dismantle our reliance upon our own righteousness and maverick abilities. This process occurs precisely when we believe we've achieved what the previous generation struggled for.

The good news is we have been in the tension of cutting away. Our hearts have been enduring deep circumcision. We are returning to holy consecration and purity and going through the "eye of the needle" in this hour. Some of what we thought was warfare was His shaking, sifting, and stripping.

His mercy cuts away the flesh that hinders love. He longs to unveil mysteries and show us His beauty. It's essential to remember that our reward isn't merely the gifts of the Spirit, but rather, knowing Him.

In the past, Egypt's gold was misused to create a golden calf, which had to be destroyed. Now grace is our gold that delivers and empowers us to live in holiness. May we never abuse this grace. It provides for us even in the darkest moments, breaking us free from wandering.

His grace rescues us from false teachings and religious bondage, opening our eyes to the truth. These teachings and revelations are intended to help us remain pure, cross over into His presence, and become His dwelling place. Let our grace not become material by which we build a new idol, lest He flips our transactional tables. Instead, let's restore holy tables for feasting on Him, honoring the sacrifice of His blood, and transforming our lives, homes, and churches into holy houses of prayer that can bear with Him in the hour of testing. Let us be bold messengers who bear the Lord's burden with diligence and remain vigilant in the time leading up to His return.

LET'S ENCOUNTER

God has invited you into more, into deeper revelation and the mysteries of His garden, as you participate in restoration through intercession and become His true friend and witness. Are you willing to release yourself to Him and bow low so that the King of Glory may enter? Ask for greater revelation of the power of the Lamb of God. Learn to behold Him as He teaches you His ways. Give Him false burdens, whatever is holding you back, in exchange for the mission of tarrying with Him in this hour. Ask Him to restore the table of intimacy in your life, family, and church. Let no personal aspiration, hesitation, or earthly protocol stamp out your fire to be an intercessor and messenger in this critical time.

PRAY WITH ME

Dear Lord, help me to be bold and brave as I surrender all I am to know your glory. Fill my mouth, heart, and mind with revelation and understanding of your intercessions for this age, but also deliver me from leaning on my human understanding. I know there is more you want to show me about you and your kingdom. I say, "Here I am, Lord. I surrender. I want to know you and be your messenger in both prayer and word." Amen.

12

COMPELLED BY THE GROAN

Prayer is not a discourse. It's a form of life, the life with God. That is why it is not confined to the moment of a verbal statement. The latter can only be a secondary expression of a relationship with God, an overflow from the encounter between the living God and the living person.

—Jacques Ellul

Some would say that all I've known is sacrifice, while others would proclaim I've accomplished much. I would say I've learned that building and walking with God looks more like giving away, tearing down, and letting go than staking a claim that something *belongs* to me.

My dad is a businessman. He used to repeat the common truism, "Everything is for sale if the price is right." In a sense, he held nothing too closely. Letting something go was never counted as a loss if there was a more significant provision in store for our family.

Messengers in the kingdom of God obtain heavenly treasures by intentionally releasing everything of lesser value. Actually, they willingly *sell it all to buy the field.* The most important treasure we can hold on to is the blessing of knowing Him. Worldly successes, ministry, or what we have built throughout life are pleasures given to the one who follows Christ. As His lovers, we then repeatedly lay these down, removing anything that impedes proximity to Him. As we seek Him, there is no loss.

> Again, the kingdom of heaven is like a merchant seeking beautiful pearls, who, when he had found one pearl of great price, went and sold all that he had and bought it.
>
> —Matthew 13:45–46 NKJV

The Treasure in the Field

Giving up our dream often looks like death, but God always resurrects our greatest sacrifice with increased kingdom fruitfulness. Anointing is produced through crushing and pressing. Glory in us is formed through suffering.

I dream of hosting the presence of God and raising an army of messengers for His glory. I've come alongside others in planting ministries, planted my own, and traveled the nation implementing this dream. I've experienced unbelievable levels of His glory in meetings. Like David of old, I strategize such a ministry's spiritual and physical measurements. I long to live all the days of my life in prayer, worship, going into the world preaching the Gospel, and coming home to pour into spiritual sons and daughters. All these things are wonderful and, indeed, His desires. He places within each of us a longing to fulfill the Great Commission.

Doing the dream of God is glorious, but there are hard-hitting attacks. God births sons and daughters from the intensity of His thick presence, and we taste authentic revival. I hold the form lightly; the Spirit of the Lord is leading. This allows the movement to evolve, looking more like Him than me.

After my encounter in Israel, He asked me to give the House of Prayer/Revival Hub that I had planted back to Him. He told me to close the doors and move my family to be near the International House of Prayer in Atlanta, Georgia. Just when we were finally getting consistent local traction, the Lord told me to lay it down. He ordered the closure three months before the 2020 COVID-19 pandemic. I didn't know what the next two years would hold, but God did.

First Samuel 15:22 says, "Obedience is better than sacrifice" (BSB). But don't underestimate obedience; it is always costly. A lifestyle of radical submission to the smallest whisper of the Holy Spirit will anger the legalistic and terrify the control freak. Operating in the freedom to hold temporary things loosely *enrages* the enemy. Left to a religious spirit, the unrestrained become captive again.

The Lord's work is mighty. The cost is tremendous; tears are my bread day and night in some seasons, but joy always comes. A river always springs up from dry places. For years, obedience, sacrifice, and brokenness became familiar to my soul, but my delight remained in Him. In the night seasons, He forms the brightness of His glory in us.

In the prayer room in Atlanta, I wept in intercession more often than not. I would ask God to remove the so-called gift of tears, and then, when I felt *normal*, I would shout, "No, I'm sorry. I want to feel what you feel. Give the weeping back. If tears birth awakening, *I'll cry forever!*" But years of tears get a little annoying, to be honest. He formed a glory superior to what I could ask or think.

Tears of Power

"Jesus wept." Simple words, yet powerful tears. In John 11:35, we are witnessing the power of travail. Wordless pants and sighs came upon Him. Did He feel the injustice of death reaping those dear to Him? Was He touching the throne with His weeping? What I do know is that *He was groaning in that passage of Scripture.*

Jesus invites us to enter that suffering with Him. Do we see the intersection of heaven and earth in His intense lack of speech? One version translates John 11:35 as "Jesus burst into tears" (ISV).

Could this be an eyewitness account of Yeshua's spiritually violent compassion and desire for justice as He falls to His knees in prayer? Could the word *wept* here actually mean "prayed without words, only tears," like the language of Romans 8:26? We could interpret the passage as "the mouth of Jesus moved, but no words came out, only groans and tears." Wordless pants and sighs came upon our Savior. He translated His breath and tears with a statement to those who accompanied Him so that our Father would be glorified.

Jesus exhaled the power of resurrection in the moments that followed. His weeping released authority that conquered death with three words: "Lazarus, come forth." I imagine God exhaling from the inner being of the Son of Man with a boom that shook all who were there to witness. Did the ground tremble? Did the bones of Lazarus shake as he was awakened? Did everyone's hair stand up as the dead man walked out of the tomb?

I am convinced the power of the resurrection is directly linked to humility produced from tears. Compassion is created in this weeping intercession when we pause, feel, and allow the moment to grip us. Consider this powerful mystery: Jesus identifies with shattered humanity and is willing to cry with us, within us, and for us.

Simply stand in awe. His intentional pause and subsequent groaning unleashed the breath of life. God healed my daughter on her deathbed. The weeping of Jesus and His groan release the power to raise the dead and turn a generation back to God. A cry transformed death into resurrection life.

Consider His invitation when He whispers to your heart, "Will you tarry with me in this hour?"

Glory Carriers and Living Stones

The emerging remnant of consecrated intercessors boldly carries the glory of the Lord during times of suffering. These will not yield to the fear of man but will be relentlessly obedient to His whisper. They have learned the beauty of dwelling with Him in prayer. They aren't afraid of tears, groans, silence, loud shouts, and the like. These bold ones are willing to endure suffering with Him; they know that greater glory is being formed in them.

He is their joy, and His joy is their strength. Abiding is their lifestyle, and they love it. Like the disciples of Jesus in Luke 19:40, they will open their mouths even if it costs them their reputations or lives. His love presses them onward. They are the living stones that have learned to minister as priests before Him (1 Peter 2:5). Their voices echo in the heavens, releasing His power to invade the earth.

> And yet some of the Pharisees in the crowd said to Him, "Teacher, rebuke Your disciples!" Jesus replied, "I tell you, if these stop speaking, the stones will cry out!"
>
> —Luke 19:39–40

Jesus's reference to the stones crying out in this passage was a prophecy. The ancient Jews referred to Gentiles in a derogatory way as dirt or dogs, but Jesus is expressing their value as voices who will cry out in worship to Him. Jesus was pointing to them as the material He would use to build His kingdom. The word in Greek is *lithos,* a noun used to describe Jesus in 1 Peter 2:7 as the chief cornerstone and the living stones in Romans 9:33 from which the temple of God is built.[1] In 1 Peter 2:5, these costly stones of truth build the church.

In essence, Jesus was rebuking His chosen for silencing the voices of their own and was warning them of the coming age in which the Gentiles would provoke them to jealousy. Beloved, Jesus was not talking about rocks singing worship songs. He was talking about you and me being used to build His prevailing Church, because we are white-hot in love with Him and grafted into the eternal family of God.

He prophesied that you and I would bear His cross with Him and lead the charge of releasing the knowledge of His glory to cover the earth as the waters cover the sea at the end of the age. I probably just ruined one of your favorite worship songs, but when you sing, "I Won't Let the Rocks Cry Out," you are fulfilling the prophecy and prophesying at the same time. You'd better cry out. You better use your voice because if you don't, you are like those who rejected Jesus the Messiah at His first coming.

You Are a Jewel and a Priest unto Him

As you come to Him, the living stone, rejected by men but chosen and precious in God's sight, you also, like living stones, are being built into a spiritual house to be a holy priesthood, offering spiritual sacrifices acceptable to God through Jesus Christ. For it stands in Scripture: "See, I lay a stone in Zion, a chosen and precious cornerstone, and the one who trusts in him will never be put to shame" (1 Peter 2:6 NIV).

Now He is building up a place for us; we have His Spirit so that we may be filled with God's very emotions. It's time we take our seat with Him and do the work of releasing His kingdom. He is the Chief Cornerstone that the builders re-jected, but also, the Builder and the Architect is building an eternal city.

We are the living stones of which He prophesied, liber-ated from the fear of man and our inclination to conform to the chaos of culture. We have a job to do with our relentless Savior. Our work is done from the throne room, not from a place of anxiety and fear. Remember, we are seated with Him in heavenly places above all enemy warfare, so take your rightful place and enforce His win (Ephesians 1:20; 2:6).

Wailing, lamenting, and suffering in Him and by His side is a gift. Perhaps it's not as painful as we anticipated. Grief mingled with longing is palpable, yet we have hope. Similar to Paul, we can regard relationships and what we've given up as a loss in exchange for gaining knowledge of Him and dwelling in His presence. We have been misinterpreted and ridiculed; some have even lost ministerial positions and jobs. Others have lost friends, children, spouses, and family members to death due to demonic fiery trials and persecutions. Many have experienced loss in one area of life while simultaneously see-ing the glory of God, healing, and prodigals coming home in another. Suffering and glory are mysteriously both bitter and sweet in this life.

These experiences have unveiled greater treasure and kin-dled a fiercer faith within us. As we give away this earthly life and obtain our eternal dwelling in Him, we become akin to the believers described in Hebrews 11: "Women received back their dead by resurrection; and others were tortured, not accepting their release, so that they might obtain a better resurrection" (Hebrews 11:35).

Perhaps you haven't yet faced the loss of life, but I'm sure you've endured painful trials due to your faith. We all do. Maybe you picked up this book because you're beginning to sense the fire of God and your passion for Him is intensifying. You seek reassurance that you're not alone; that holy dissatisfaction serves a purpose. Have you been challenged to weigh the cost? There's more in store for you. Cry out to Him now, "Father, do not hold back. I want more! I recognize how much more I need to discover about you."

As your eyes fill with holy tears and your heart begins to beat as His presence arrives, read on. You are about to be driven from where you were before you picked up this book. Many have felt like a horse in a race, waiting behind a gate. Frustration has driven us to release wordless groans of prayer, like the cries of barren Hannah. Burning one, the Lord is now shouting, "Burst forth and run with wild abandon."

This divine inner drive of the Holy Spirit's groan is flawlessly described with the Greek word *ekballō*.[2] By His hand, He propels us beyond the confines of four walls, shaping us into bold messengers. He is shifting people from church pews and prayer rooms to the vast global harvest fields. This divine commissioning is beyond explanation; it must be personally experienced. The inner witness beckons you to simply go, to manifest the glory of Jesus, the true Messiah, and to stand against the prevailing spirit of the age, even if it means giving your life (2 Peter 3:3–8). The deeper you abide in Him, the more the drive will increase.

Answering *Ekballō*

Many in the prayer movement have been praying Matthew 9:38 for the Lord of the harvest to send forth laborers into the fields, but when He begins driving people out of the four walls, we are shocked. He is not interested in submitting to our compartmentalized thinking of readiness, locations, spiritual times, carnal seasons, and careers. Spiritually, as when autumn turns to winter, the days of freedom to proclaim Jesus are getting shorter; therefore, the Lord is sending.

Fear must not be figured in our equation when dispatching those who burn with His fire into the hardest and darkest places of the earth. They blaze with the light of His glory and carry the message of the hour. They will continue to be equipped while obedient. The inward compelling is accelerating growth and revelation of the Second Coming of Jesus. Simultaneously, the accuser is breeding excuses to stop or hinder missionaries. Mocking, false doctrines, persecution, political drama, wars, and intimidation attempt to derail the launch of holy witnesses. Mocking has always been and will continue. The fear of man must break—the Holy Spirit is groaning.

> Above all, you must understand that in the last days scoffers will come, scoffing and following their own evil desires. They will say, "Where is this 'coming' he promised? Ever since our ancestors died, everything goes on as it has since the beginning of creation." But they deliberately forget that long ago by God's word the heavens came into being and the earth was formed out of water and by water. By these waters also the world of that time was deluged and destroyed. By the same word the present heavens and earth are reserved for fire, being kept for the day of judgment and destruction

223

of the ungodly. Do not forget this one thing, dear friends: With the Lord a day is like a thousand years, and a thousand years are like a day.

—2 Peter 3:3–8 NIV

Are you beginning to understand His *ekballo* in you? Have you been afraid of being mocked when you start to roar? Has intimidation had you hiding in the cave? Have you been waiting for permission to go? Stop fearing; you have *holy grit*.

The Grand Invitation

His invitation shouts to the hearts of men, women, and children, to all who will listen. "Come. I will show you the mysteries and give you heaven's strategies for the time in which you live." The call to ascend the hill of the Lord is now. The urgency and warning are like the warning in Matthew. We must not harden our hearts as some have, for we are living in the very days prophesied, and "as it was in the days of Noah, so it will be in the coming of the Son of Man" (Matthew 24:37 NIV).

Those who choose to harden their hearts and resist His calling will soon get the delusion they desire. Many are called, and few are chosen. Beloved, this is a glorious calling: "Come up here! Come out from among them and be consecrated. Will you walk as a priest before me and do the work of a king in the earth even until the end of the age?"

The same invitation was given to Moses, Elijah, Enoch, John the Baptist, and John the Beloved—even now, calling and commissioning is being discharged from the throne of God to you. Would you like to be a witness of His matchless glory? He is faithful to His Word. You will see Him. You will know His ways. He will go with you. Simply abide in Him and yield fully to Him. Trust Him in His kindness and severity. "The present suffering is nothing compared to the coming glory that is going to be revealed to us" (Romans 8:18 CEB).

Holy Dissatisfaction

I thought the wordless groan would eventually end. It was as if my goal was to satisfy the longing for justice and perfection before the Second Coming of the Lord. As I type these words, I realize that subconscious narrative is impossible. Your dissatisfaction with less than His fullness in the earth is holy. He will incline to groan within you as the holy frustration drives you to become a consecrated voice in these final days. As you refuse spiritual mixture with ungodliness, you will move in the authority and power of God, but it will not come uncontested. It will be challenged more than you ever thought possible.

If you don't quit, you win. He never stops making intercession for us. His blood still cries out, and His groan will not cease until the fullness of Gentiles come to Him, Israel receives Him, creation acquires redemption, and His bride is married. He never ceases; He has already won.

The Unlikely Messengers Are Coming. Guys, Listen Up.

> Now after He had risen early on the first day of the week, He first appeared to Mary Magdalene, from whom He had cast out seven demons. She went and reported to those who had been with Him, while they were mourning and weeping. And when they heard that He was alive and had been seen by her, they refused to believe it.
>
> —Mark 16:9–11

God loves to use unlikely messengers. I find it powerfully interesting that God not only used a woman but a woman delivered of seven demons in an era when women were not considered credible witnesses. Still, Jesus invited her to bring the first resurrection report to His skeptical disciples. These had witnessed her kiss and anoint the feet of Jesus with costly ointment and her refusal to be unmoved by judgmental rebukes. Untouched by the condemnation and reactions of men, this woman was the epitome of *holy grit*. She followed Him to the cross and the tomb and was the first to see Him resurrected. But the guys still did not listen to her when she told them, "He has risen!"

Lovesick hunger is for Him alone. He reveals Himself to His friends and shares His mysteries with them. Don't think for a moment that modern-day wailing women have lost their minds when they proclaim, "He's coming! He's here!" He is increasing a mighty multitude of women in this hour and moving through the most unlikely vessels. "The Lord gives the word; the women who announce the news are a great host" (Psalm 68:11 ESV).

His daughters are relentless in seeking His face, even if it demands everything. Their sobbing message may sound emotional, but it carries an encounter with His glory. In this hour of darkness, let's not repeat the disciples' mistake when they were so overwhelmed by circumstances that they couldn't hear the message of His resurrection delivered by an emotional woman. At this crucial time, men and women must unite. His voice is needed, her voice is needed. Think about this: Without Mordecai's lament and galvanizing voice, Esther would not have found the courage to speak out, resulting in no audience with the king and the possible massacre of the Jews. Their partnership was lifesaving.

He's ready to unlock profound encounters beyond our wildest dreams as we plunge into tears, travail, and intercession. The preparation for greater glory is underway. Unlikely one, prepare to rise into a deeper dimension of God. Let not your hearts be troubled; He has conquered the world. He's ushering in an awakening and intensifying His presence.

His arrival is imminent, but first, He awakens His downtrodden, weeping, mourning messengers. He will send out those who have become living testimonies as authoritative alarm clocks brimming with unwavering joy. Their joy doesn't align with darkness or the enemy's accusations but exposes them. They discern the signs and grasp the spiritual times and seasons, yet refuse to credit the serpent. They put that lair under their feet. They have that dauntless determination to "dare, and dare until they die," like Joan of Arc. They have seen and heard and stand ready to lay down their lives.[3]

Recommission Those in Unbelief

> Later He appeared to the eleven disciples themselves as they were reclining at the table; and He reprimanded them for their unbelief and hardness of heart, because they had not believed those who had seen Him after He had risen from the dead.
>
> —Mark 16:14

Can you see the prophetic masterpiece? I can see Him there, standing in the doorway. He has a smile of adulation. Like a loving Father, He watches them for a moment. They are weeping, dirty, exhausted, and maybe even hungry. Mary and the other witnesses look up and see Him, shrugging their shoulders as if to say, "We tried to tell them."

Then the eleven look up, eyes practically popping out of their heads. They gasp, and He speaks: "Hi, guys! Why do you still disregard Mary? I knew you wouldn't listen, so I sent two others." Their grief becomes tears of joy mixed with faith, laughter, and holy sobbing. They are vexed by the gap between what was promised and what was shattered. But then He walked in; Jesus always terminates a void with His presence.

Simply Open Your Mouth and Go

He said to them, "Go into all the world and preach the gospel to all creation. Whoever believes and is baptized will be saved, but whoever does not believe will be condemned. And these signs will accompany those who believe: In my name they will drive out demons; they will speak in new tongues; they will pick up snakes with their hands; and when they drink deadly poison, it will not hurt them at all; they will place their hands on sick people, and they will get well."

—Mark 16:15–18 NIV

In one of my favorite commissioning passages (above), Jesus quickly re-establishes His disciples in their mission. As you read the Scriptures, may your eyes open to yourself, your family, your church, and your nation in this storyline. Consecrated witnesses are the only thing standing between the Church and the antichrist agenda. Your mouth is your weapon in heaven and on earth, so open it.

The most beautiful part of all is that you are never alone. You are seated with Him, and you have been given His authority. He has been with you and will demonstrate His fame for the glory of His name forever. "And they went out and preached everywhere, while the Lord worked with them, and confirmed the word by the signs that followed" (Mark 16:20).

Lean into the Groan

It's a co-mission, beloved. The Faithful Witness who has revealed Himself is with you in the wailing, pain, persecution, and void. He is there when you look death in the face, but He is also in joy, laughter, and days of plenty. He's still alive to intercede and eager to show you His glory. (See Romans 8:35–39.)

Lean into the groan and zeal for His house. Unspoken mysteries are being unveiled as you journey with Him. Stay faithful to the end. He loves you so deeply. Nothing can separate you from His love. Remain uncompromising in your message, faithful to prayer, and awestruck by His face. Believe there will be healing, deliverance, setting free of the captives, and raising of the dead.

You've endured painful oppression, spiritual warfare, and religious attacks. The suffering you've borne has been instrumental in shaping your identity and the power of your intercessions. As you've waited in humility, greater glory is being unveiled, eclipsing the hardships you've endured. This moment is awaited with anticipation by all of creation.

LET'S ENCOUNTER

Our faith increases as we press past the travail of frustration and learn to trust the Lord's faithfulness to use our weakness.

His goal is simple: He's looking for friends who will make themselves His house of prayer; He is looking for those with whom He can unveil His secrets and give His authority. But God awakens spiritual senses through holy frustration. You are not only an intercessor or one with a burden of prayer; you are a mouthpiece that speaks and an ear that hears. More importantly, as you learn to calm your inner man, you can see what He is doing, taste and see His goodness, feel His joy, and even smell the aroma of His presence in the room where you sit.

We are vessels holding unseen, unheard, and yet-to-be-revealed glory. There's an abundance waiting for us as we embrace the eternal life He has won for us, even in this earthly realm. As His voice beckons us beyond the toil of prayer, our hearts must be readied to respond to our tears and groans by going forth into the harvest. We embody the message and intercessions of the Lamb. The groaning continues, yet the burden becomes lighter as we partake in the glorious stealth mission, acting as spiritual snipers and laser-accurate love bombers. When we speak, words are oracles that shake the darkness and set captives free.

PRAY WITH ME

Thank you, God, that trusting you moves me from the realm of the flesh into the realms only accessible by abiding in you. Thank you for changing my desires and worldview through my groans. I know I can live in the world but not of it when I resist the urge of the flesh to fret over the evil of this world and instead awaken others back to you. I know my tears, groans, and words matter, and by abiding in you, I will speak oracles, not curses or complaints. I will fast,

I will pray, I will groan, I will declare, I will gaze, I will abide, and I will go. Keep my eyes locked on you, for now I know you hear and answer my groans and tears. Here am I, Lord; send me. May the Lamb receive the reward of His suffering. Amen.

NOTES

Chapter 1 Unspoken Intercession

1. "John Chau Martyred On North Sentinel Island," The Voice of the Martyrs, June 4, 2022, https://www.persecution.com/stories/john-chau.

2. "Meaning of Numbers in the Bible: The Number 7," BibleStudy.org, accessed November 5, 2023, https://www.biblestudy.org/bibleref/meaning-of-numbers-in-bible/7.html.

Chapter 2 Gripped by the Groan

1. "Strong's #3140: martureo," BibleTools.org, accessed November 5, 2023, https://www.bibletools.org/index.cfm/fuseaction/Lexicon.show/ID/G3140/martureo.htm; "Romans 8:16," BibleHub.com, accessed November 5, 2023, https://biblehub.com/text/romans/8-16.htm.

2. "3144. Martus," in *Strong's Concordance*, BibleHub.com, accessed November 5, 2023, https://biblehub.com/greek/3144.htm.

3. "Dr. Martin Luther King, Jr. Speech at Illinois Wesleyan University, 1966," Illinois Wesleyan University, accessed November 5, 2023, https://www.iwu.edu/mlk/page-5.html.

4. Bob Jones quoted in Corey Russell, *The Gift of Tears* (Lewisville, TX: Nasharite Publishing, 2021), 60.

5. "Topical Studies: What the Bible says about Apocalypto (From *Forerunner Commentary*)," BibleTools.org, accessed November 5, 2023, https://www.bibletools.org/index.cfm/fuseaction/Topical.show/RTD/cgg/ID/5382/Apocalypto.htm.

Chapter 3 Holy Burden Carriers

1. Leonard Ravenhill, *Revival Praying* (Minneapolis, MN: Bethany Fellowship, 1980), 61–62.

2. Charles Haddon Spurgeon, "The Burden of the Word of the Lord," The Spurgeon Center, accessed November 5, 2023, https://www.spurg eon.org/resource-library/sermons/the-burden-of-the-word-of-the-lord /#flipbook/.

Chapter 4 You Have History with God

1. A.W. Tozer, ed. James L. Snyder, *The Pursuit of God: The Definitive Classic* (Minneapolis, MN: Bethany House Publishers, 2020), 27.
2. "G5550 - chronos - Strong's Greek Lexicon (kjv)," Blue Letter Bible, accessed November 5, 2023, https://www.blueletterbible.org/lexicon /g5550/kjv/tr/0-1/; "G2540 - kairos - Strong's Greek Lexicon (kjv)," Blue Letter Bible, accessed November 5, 2023, https://www.blueletterbible.org /lexicon/g2540/kjv/tr/0-1/.

Chapter 5 Tipping Heavenly Bowls

1. Corey Russell, *Teach Us to Pray: Prayer That Accesses Heaven and Changes Earth* (Shippensburg, PA: Destiny Image, 2020), 38.
2. Taylor Berglund, "Homecoming," *Charisma Magazine*, November 2019, 30–31, https://issuu.com/charismamediaproduction/docs/cm1119_dig.

Chapter 6 The Unseen War

1. Laura Hanrahan, "60 'Elf' Quotes That'll Give You All the Christmas Cheer," *Cosmopolitan*, December 2, 2022, https://www.cosmopolitan.com /entertainment/movies/a38193153/best-elf-quotes/.
2. Arthur Wallis, *In the Day of Thy Power: The Scriptural Principles of Revival* (London: Christian Literature Crusade, 1961), 14.

Chapter 8 There's a Sword in Your Mouth

1. Norman Grubb, *Rees Howells: Intercessor* (Cambridge: Lutterworth Press, 1978), 97–8.
2. Ibid.
3. Ibid.
4. "1827. demamah," in Strong's Concordance, BibleHub.com, accessed November 5, 2023, https://biblehub.com/hebrew/1827.htm.

Chapter 9 Eyes to See Beyond

1. "Article #7: Fourscore and six years have I served him, and he has never done me injury," Christian History Institute, accessed November 5, 2023, https://christianhistoryinstitute.org/incontext/article/polycarp-testimony.
2. Ibid.
3. Ibid.

4. Randy Alcorn, "Josef Tson: What His Suffering for Christ in Communist Romania Taught Him, and Can Teach Us," Church Leaders, July 5, 2022, https://churchleaders.com/pastors/428008-josef-tson-what-his-suffering-for-christ-in-communist-romania-taught-him-and-can-teach-us.html.

5. "Brooke Wells," No Bull Project, June 29, 2021, https://www.nobull project.com/blogs/crossfit athletes/brooke-wells.

Chapter 10 Waiting on the Weight of Glory

1. R.C. Sproul, "Trembling Before the Holiness of God," Ligonier, February 27, 2019, https://www.ligonier.org/posts/trembling-holiness-god.

Chapter 12 Compelled by the Groan

1. *"Elliott's Commentary for English Readers*, 1 Peter 2:4," Bible Hub, accessed November 6, 2023, https://biblehub.com/commentaries/1_peter/2-4.htm.

2. "G1544 - ekballō - Strong's Greek Lexicon (kjv)," Blue Letter Bible, accessed November 6, 2023, https://www.blueletterbible.org/lexicon/g1544/kjv/tr/0-1/.

3. George Bernard Shaw, Dan H. Laurence, Imogen Stubbs, *Saint Joan: A Chronicle Play in Six Scenes and an Epilogue* (New York: Penguin Publishing Group, 2001), 111.

Podcaster, author, fiery preacher, and Jesus-lover **Tammie Southerland** longs to raise up a generation of consecrated, blazing intercessors and bold messengers in the final hours before Jesus's return. With passion and a deep prophetic understanding of the times, she equips believers with the necessary tools and knowledge to impact their communities and make disciples. Her podcast, books, and teachings inspire people to be fearless ambassadors for Christ.

She founded and leads Burning Ones Academy and Frontline Ministries International, a global media, mobile prayer, and fivefold ministry-equipping hub that helps people around the world impact their homes, regions, and nations with intercession, worship, revival fire, and discipleship. She orchestrates intercession, worship, online podcasts, courses, and gatherings with boots-on-the-ground meetings to help bridge the gap between house churches, the prayer movement, the underground Church, and local churches worldwide.

Tammie plumb-lines, connects, and galvanizes burning messengers from all backgrounds who want to serve Jesus. An apostolic and house of prayer leader in her local church north of Atlanta, Tammie is working with other Atlanta leaders to establish a Kingdom Revival Hub where Christian media, music, gatherings, and trainings impact the nations.

Tammie's prophetic voice, passion for authentic revival, and moving people to God's fullness have made her a sought-after international speaker. Her heart is to restore hungry, weary people and burned-out leaders to first-love intimacy with God.

Tammie and her husband, Daymon, live in the Atlanta area with their three daughters, Eden, Jayden, and Adley. For more information, podcasts, media, gatherings, and course enrollment, visit TammieSoutherland.org.